Managing
Lean
Projects

Managing
Lean
Projects

Ralph L. Kliem, PMP, CBCP

CRC Press
Taylor & Francis Group
Boca Raton London New York

CRC Press is an imprint of the
Taylor & Francis Group, an **Informa** business
AN AUERBACH BOOK

CRC Press
Taylor & Francis Group
6000 Broken Sound Parkway NW, Suite 300
Boca Raton, FL 33487-2742

Printed on acid-free paper
Version Date: 20150901

International Standard Book Number-13: 978-1-4822-5182-1 (Hardback)

Visit the Taylor & Francis Web site at
http://www.taylorandfrancis.com

and the CRC Press Web site at
http://www.crcpress.com

For my two college buddies, Jim Davis, who recently passed away, and Drew Powers. I will always value our friendship and the great times we had. Thanks for the memories and comradeship.

Contents

Preface

Sometimes revolutions come with a burst of energy, shaking up the world dramatically. At other times, they arrive in subtle ways. Lean is a revolution that is more of the latter. Like a good after-dinner liqueur, the effects hit gradually, changing one's perceptions and feelings.

Lean is a revolutionary way of changing how a private or public organization does business, whether at the strategic or operational levels. It changes how decisions are made. It changes how people interact as much as how materials are acquired, processed, and delivered. It changes the priorities by placing the customer in the forefront of everyone's minds. Above all, it creates as much as it destroys. The last thing one wants in any revolution, even in business, is to devour one's own children.

Project management is a means to prevent, or at least to soften the impact of, the Lean revolution. It provides the discipline needed to harness the energy and power that Lean offers so that everyone benefits from the gains, despite the pain that often accompanies it. Fortunately, I have been the beneficiary of those gains, such as higher stock prices and greater bonuses. I have also, sorrowfully, found myself a victim of Lean and other process improvement efforts. Success came, but only after falling on my own sword. Yes, Lean can not only devour its own children but its parents, too. I've seen people lose their livelihoods while others enriched their own pockets without any consequence, just as in most revolutions.

Project management plays a significant role because it is not just about building schedules, collecting data, using software applications, and maintaining costs. It is also about people. In fact, it is all about people. If applied, project management can serve as a means to obtain ownership and commitment among everyone at all levels of an organization, from the chief executive officer to the rank and file on an assembly line. It can also open everyone's vision and perceptions about the reason why an organization exists in the first place. It can help everyone to participate effectively, not just efficiently, in satisfying the customer. It helps absorb the pain, and spread the gain, from a Lean project.

This book is not a diatribe about Lean although it does discuss some of the major concepts and techniques that make it so powerful. Rather, its purpose is to help project professionals to apply and leverage the power of their field to help them lead, not just manage, their Lean projects to success and to the benefit of their organization and the people who work in it.

Acknowledgment

I want to thank my personal editor, Ameeta Chainani, for taking the time to review the manuscript and to provide insights on improving it.

About the Author

Ralph L. Kliem, PMP, CBCP, president of LeanPM, LLC, has more than 30 years of experience with Fortune 500 firms, including Safeco Insurance Companies and The Boeing Company.

Ralph started his business career as methods analyst for Safeco Insurance Companies, performing time and motion studies and executing process improvement responsibilities for an information technology department. Later, as a senior project manager with The Boeing Company, he managed several process improvement, maturity model, and Lean projects. Ralph was the project manager for the companywide re-engineering of The Boeing Company's policies and procedures process during and after the merger with McDonnell Douglas. He was also the project manager for information technology projects that supported the 787 and P8A programs; several of these projects had the purpose of achieving specific maturity levels according to Software Engineering Institute's Capability Maturity Model Integration (CMMI) model. As a corporate internal auditor, he also led several process improvement projects, one of which evaluated the effectiveness of direct shipment and transition to just-in-time delivery of paints to the 777 program. He also led numerous audit projects that evaluated the performance of other major business and information technology projects and programs including some for Boeing's Executive Council and Audit Committee. Ralph was also the project manager for a Lean initiative that improved the business continuity processes supporting several of the major airplane programs such as the 747, 767, 777, and 787, and major business units and programs within The Boeing Company.

In addition, Ralph teaches PMP certification courses and conducts project management seminars and workshops. He is an adjunct faculty member of City University and a former member of Seattle Pacific University in Seattle, Washington. He is also an instructor with the continuing education program at Bellevue College, Cascadia Community College, and Everett Community College in Seattle, Washington. He is the author or coauthor of more than 15 books and 300 articles with leading business and information technology publications.

He can be reached at ralph.kliem@frontier.com; (206) 963-5246; or via www.theleanpm.com.

1

The Long Road to Lean

Lean did not just pop up overnight in the corporate world. It is predicated on a long legacy of other approaches that allowed it to become a reality, originating as far back as the 1980s, if not earlier.

1.1 QUALITY: A SHORT HISTORICAL PERSPECTIVE

In large part, the rise of Lean owes its existence to the Quality Movement that took on, in the 1980s and 1990s, what was known as the Japanese challenge. Much of this movement was predicated on the works of a small handful of gentlemen, mainly American, who ironically seemed to receive more fanfare outside the United States than in it. See Figure 1.1.

One of the first names in the Quality Movement in the United States is Philip Crosby. His major contribution to the Quality Movement was conformance to requirements. The idea was that whatever was delivered to the customer must conform to business and design specifications, and be as determined by the customer and other standards. He also stressed the concept of zero defects and discussed at length the impact of poor quality as well as the importance of prevention over inspection by ensuring that no defective product or service is delivered to the customer. He coined the concept "quality isn't free," meaning that achieving quality requires an investment that must lead to returns. Ideally, he observed that a point of equilibrium is reached between the benefits of investing in quality measures and the costs; ideally, the payback gets greater for every dollar invested.

Ironically, W. Edwards Deming became a legend in the Quality Movement in the United States long after he had become one in Japan.

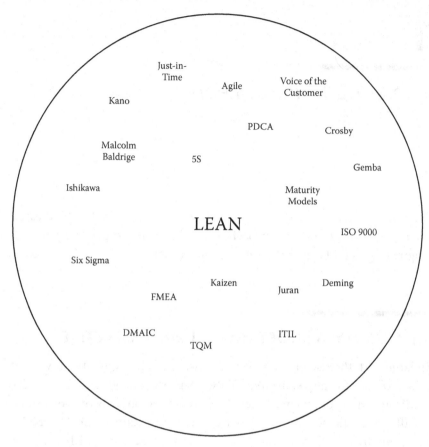

FIGURE 1.1
The dynamic world of quality.

He advocated taking a systemic perspective regarding quality and emphasized the need for statistical analysis as a basis for achieving quality. He identified his famous 14 Steps of Quality which essentially advocate adopting quality as a philosophy that emphasizes the importance of it being in the forefront of everyone's minds, taking ownership and responsibility for the quality of work up and down the organizational hierarchy, the existing need to eliminate psychological as well as physical barriers to quality, and providing everyone with the knowledge and other support to ensure quality is built from within and not inspected from without. Deming also adopted the formula, plan, do, check, act (PDCA), often erroneously referred to as the Deming wheel, for making improvements.

Joseph Juran is another legend in the Quality Movement. Like Deming, he received considerable acceptance in Japan before receiving widespread recognition in the United States. He is noted for giving quality a more humanistic perspective and he embraced the concept of "fitness for use" and "conformance to requirements." The former stresses the importance of delivering or producing a product or delivering a service that meets certain requirements; the latter is that the product or service satisfies real needs. Another key concept that he advocated is the Pareto rule which essentially says that 80% of the effects are the result of 20% of the causes.

Crosby, Deming, and Juran represent the triple crown of the Quality Movement in the United States. It was their contributions, not the only ones, however, that laid the basis for the Total Quality Management, or TQM. During the 1980s, especially, TQM provided an organizational approach to quality. The basic approach was to form what were known as quality circles, consisting of a cross-functional group of people, working to solve quality problems or to improve processes, resulting in customer satisfaction. The group would apply a wide array of quality tools and techniques to define the problem or issue and then come up with one or more recommendations. Many of these tools and techniques were developed by Japanese quality experts. In large organizations, it was not unusual for an employee at any level in an organization to participate in multiple quality circles.

TQM was one of the first organizational initiatives to improve quality in organizations. Since that time, there have also been several others that either have capitalized on TQM or risen in parallel to it.

Six Sigma, originating with Motorola, is a statistical approach applied toward managing variation in processes that lead to defects. It relies on a series of statistical tools and techniques that provide greater reliability in the product or service being delivered to the customer. The idea is to reduce variability around the mean, or average, as well as meet the specifications as defined by the customer. Six Sigma basically means that 99.99966% of the output of a process is defect free; as such, it depends on heavy use of statistical methods to determine the appropriate level of quality to achieve; it requires constant monitoring to determine whether that appropriate level of quality has been met and applying the PDCA cycle to determine the effectiveness of a change, for example, and making any necessary adjustments.

Six Sigma has managed to merge, to some degree, with Lean, creating a hybrid known as Lean Six Sigma. Unlike Six Sigma, the focus shifts entirely to the customer. It requires looking at the value stream from both an As-Is and To-Be perspective and then coming up with a series of recommendations for quality improvement. The idea is to remove variation in the flow of the process stream by eliminating waste. Lean Six Sigma relies on continuous improvement as with Six Sigma. The difference is that a modified approach is adopted. The phases in the cycle increase in number and are referred to in an acronym, DMAIC, standing for define, measure, analyze, improve, and control, for improving an existing process. For a new process, the approach is DMADV, which stands for define, measure, analyze, design, and verify.

Failure mode and effects analysis, or FMEA, is another way to identify and address errors in a process, product, or service being delivered to the customer. This approach is somewhat dated in comparison with Six Sigma and Lean Six Sigma. However, some of its concepts have laid the groundwork for risk management and quality as it exists today. FMEA is basically an approach to determine and improve the reliability of a system, be it hardware, software, or process. A hierarchical perspective is taken of all the components as they are exploded into finer detail. An analysis of the components is conducted to determine failure "modes," and to identify the corresponding causes and effects. The entire effort is documented and recorded prior to a system being built. Risk mitigation is employed to deal with any threats to the components of a system. FMEA lays the basis to develop testing criteria. FMEA contributes to the Quality Movement chiefly by providing a way to ascertain threats, such as those related to poor quality in systems design, mainly hardware.

Just-in-time, or JIT, delivery has also contributed to the Quality Movement. Like FMEA, it has been around for a while. However, in the past 10 to 15 years, it has received more visibility as a means to improve customer satisfaction and to reduce operating costs. The fundamental idea behind JIT is to have timely delivery of resources to a manufacturing environment rather than have large inventories due to trying to predict future customer demand or hold large quantities for potential situations. JIT requires a steady flow of resources and information throughout a manufacturing process and today plays an integral part in the Lean process. The reason is that it depends on pull, rather than push, to meet the needs of the customer. JIT, of course, has its risks, due to the free flow of resources and a stable business environment.

Another quality initiative that occurred somewhat later is the voice of the customer, or VOC. The VOC emphasizes the importance of requirements and feedback from the customer to provide the highest level of quality possible, often referred to as best-in-class. The emphasis is on capturing user expectations, wants, and needs according to priorities established by the customer. Using qualitative and quantitative approaches both on individual and group levels, every effort is made to understand and address what the customer seeks. The VOC provides the necessary information to perform what is known in engineering disciplines as quality function deployment, or QFD, which essentially is transferring customer prioritized needs and wants into a solution.

ISO 9000 is another quality initiative that took off during the 1990s and the early 2000s. It is essentially a documentation effort that emphasizes the idea of, "Say it, do it, prove it," in an effort to meet the needs of the customer. Heavily documentation oriented, ISO 9000 has led to developing consistent quality processes within an organization as well as adhering to regulatory requirements. An independent third-party certifying organization provides the independent assessment on whether an organization is ISO 9000 compliant.

The Malcolm Baldrige Award arrived around the height of the Quality Movement in the United States, circa the late 1980s. This award, presented by the president of the United States, was coveted by manufacturing firms. The award still serves as a means to encourage firms to improve their quality practices and to select companies that serve as models for what quality should be. The winner is selected according to these criteria: leadership; strategic planning; customer focus; measurement, analysis, and knowledge management; workforce focus; operations focus; and results. The award spans six industries and has evolved from a narrow focus on quality to one of a much broader concern referred to as "performance excellence."

A number of maturity models have also arisen during the Quality Movement. Maturity models cover much more than quality. However, they can be considered an outgrowth of the Quality Movement. A maturity model consists of a level of maturity that an organization can achieve as it progresses when providing a service or building a product. Each level of maturity has criteria to satisfy before it can progress to the next highest level. The lowest level is often considered chaotic and the highest level considered highly proficient and adaptable to change. The Software Engineering Institute's Software Maturity Model, or CMM, was one of the first maturity models. CMM has evolved to CMM-I, whereby the emphasis has been on the integration of different information technology aspects. The fad for maturity models continues, but at a slower pace; models have arisen for a wide number of fields from human resource management to business continuity.

Another IT service-oriented model that focuses on quality from a customer perspective is the Information Technology Infrastructure Library, or ITIL. This model provides a series of practices related to service management. ITIL stresses the importance of alignment of services in a manner that adds value to the customer and integrates with the customer's overall strategy. Some common topics of interest include financial management; service design, operations, and improvement; business relationships; and demand management.

Around the same time as ITIL, came Agile software development. This approach toward systems development capitalized on many of the concepts of Lean. Agile relies on short delivery cycles that emphasize incremental delivery of a product, in this case software. It achieves results through a series of sprints and releases that involve close interaction with the customer as well as participation by the people doing the work. Agile was developed in response to significant lengthy cycle times for software development using the traditional life cycle approach and backlogs piling up to meet the needs of the customer. Agile also emphasizes the need for flexibility and speedier communications on the part of all the stakeholders, from the development team to the customer; however, the customer remains the focus.

Another important quality-related movement that occurred in the 1990s is re-engineering. The basic premise of re-engineering was, and still is, to overhaul workflows and business processes radically with the purpose of improving customer service, reducing costs, decreasing cycle times, and eliminating non-value-added activities. The premise is that the existing process can be overhauled with a better, ideal workflow or business process; a perfect state, so to speak. Re-engineering has received some backlash because of its perceived unrelenting war on the status quo and, consequently, less stress on incremental improvement. In many cases, re-engineering projects and initiatives involved very little participation by the people who did the work and often led to short-term results and added substantial fear among employees. Nevertheless, it required using some of the Quality Movement tools and techniques and stressed the importance of focusing on obtaining customer results.

It would be a mistake, of course, to conclude that the Quality Movement is the result of only three American gurus. The Japanese came up with some powerful concepts, tools, and techniques, too, that Americans adopted to enhance quality.

Dr. Kaoru Ishikawa is one of the leading Japanese thinkers who have contributed significantly to the Quality Movement. Not only is he the developer of the fishbone diagram, but he identified what are known as the seven quality control tools applicable to process improvement projects. The seven tools are fishbone diagrams, Pareto charts, check sheets, scatter plots, graphs, histograms, and control charts. These tools are fundamental to Lean projects. Numerous Japanese and American thinkers in the Quality Movement have leveraged these tools to supplement the originals, which also can be used on Lean projects. These tools include a wide assortment of affinity diagrams and matrices.

Another major Japanese contributor is Dr. Noriaki Kano. His contribution is showing the necessity of emphasizing the needs of the customers by understanding their requirements. He identified three categories of requirements: requirements which must be met; wants, those that the customer expects; and delighters, those that go beyond the needs and wants. Needs and wants require fulfillment; otherwise the customer will be unsatisfied. Fulfilling delighters is not necessary but can lead to a very satisfied customer.

The Japanese have also come up with several concepts that are not specifically identified with any individual, per se, but have contributed to the Quality Movement. These include kaizen for continuous improvement; the five Ss (seiri, seiton, seiso, seiketsu, and shitsuke); gemba, visiting the place of action; kanban for signaling when needing more supplies; heijunka, for leveling schedules; and many more. These concepts can be, and have been, integrated into Lean.

Japanese contributions to quality control have been immense. Their contributions have stressed the importance of focusing on the customer and minimizing obstacles through the contributions of the people doing the work. By collecting facts and data in support of improving processes and meeting the needs of the customer, they have eventually led to formulating and adopting Lean as a way of doing business. In other words, Lean is, in many respects, the pinnacle of the contributions by the Japanese and the Americans to improve quality through greater efficiency and effectiveness.

1.2 TEN TRENDS IN QUALITY

Although the above topics are by no means exhaustive, some common trends have led to Lean as we know it today (refer to Figure 1.2).

The customer is the focus of all efforts. The customer defines the expectations, wants, and needs, and it is up to the organization, such as a service provider or manufacturer, to provide products or services to define, understand, and satisfy them. The customer is literally king. All effort is geared toward satisfying the customer, whether of a product or service. Without this focus on the customer an organization is considered inefficient and ineffective in its processes, procedures, and activities that add no value other than to itself.

The organization providing the product or service must be willing to adapt to the changing requirements of the customer. The environments for both stakeholders are dynamic; ultimately, however, the organization delivering the product or service has the responsibility to adapt accordingly and to work with the customer to make any changes. These changes may involve modified functionality, demand increases or decreases, higher standards of reliability performance, or product pricing reductions, to name a few. The organization providing the product or service must be flexible to accommodate these changes.

Qualitative and quantitative variables are both important considerations to ensure that quality criteria have been met. Both variables provide a balance that should support the other. Too often the numbers become overemphasized at the expense of the qualitative criteria such as leadership, communications, and teaming. In other words, not only what is measurable is important but so are the intangible criteria. A more balanced perspective ensures the quality of the product or service being delivered to the customer.

Quality management requires taking the initiative. In other words, quality is a conscious disciplined effort. Measurements and ongoing communications, for example, must occur consistently and persistently. Quality also requires making an investment in time and effort and, like all investments, a certain point needs to be reached where the gains must at least match the losses before adding value. This initiative begins at all levels within an organization, from the very top to the very bottom of the organizational hierarchy. Ultimately, though, management retains responsibility for the quality of the output from its organization, meaning it must provide the initial impetus to encourage people to embrace quality in all

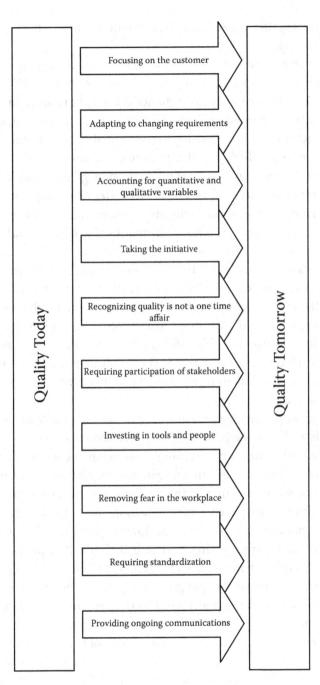

FIGURE 1.2
Trends in quality.

that they do. Quality, indeed, isn't free. It requires time, effort, and other resources to make it a reality.

Quality management is not a one-time affair. It requires continuous vigilance through feedback and monitoring. The PDCA wheel and DMAIC are two examples where continuous vigilance is needed to ensure that quality efforts on a large or small scale satisfy requirements and, if not, allow for corrective action to occur. Quality, as mentioned earlier, demands taking the initiative to get deployed. It also requires taking the initiative after deployment. Without constancy of purpose and vigilance, quality, as with any program or activity, will decline in vigor. Hence, concepts such as kaizen and customer focus serve as means to sustain quality improvement.

Quality management requires participation by affected stakeholders. Quality requires the participation of those responsible for meeting the requirements of the customer. This situation is especially the case when a cross-functional process or value stream requires improvement. The people doing the work should provide input because they have the best knowledge and expertise and have input to the recommendations for change; their buy-in is critical for successful implementation. People affected by a change will have less of an emotional commitment if they are excluded from its formulation and implementation and may actually become opponents to change.

Quality management requires investing in not only the tools to perform the work but also in the people making products and services. However, people need education and training to develop recommendations for improvement. They cannot innately generate opportunities for improvement without some investment. This training and education must be relevant and timely if they are to contribute to quality improvement.

Quality management requires removing fear in the workplace. Formulating and implementing change is difficult. It requires challenging the status quo for many reasons. Vested interests will protect themselves if they see no gain in changing. Many people become comfortable with routine and will resist any need to change unless no other choice exists. Senior leadership may see it as a threat to their power and stature within an organization. Lean, despite its claims of being incremental, can be revolutionary over time, resulting in significant change in the means of production and relationships among people. If Lean is going to work, executive leadership and senior management need to embrace change and drive fear out of the workplace. Otherwise, people will simply go through the motions and nothing will really change.

Quality management requires standardization. Common processes, tools, and techniques enable greater understanding and communication among all the participants when implementing change. Unfortunately, standardization often gets construed by some stakeholders as meaning regimentation, resulting in inflexibility and loss of creativity. Such assumptions are erroneous when it comes to collaborative efforts to produce products and services to the customer. Standardization does just the opposite, allowing for greater adaptation to change but also allowing people to operate from a common approach. Lack of standardization often results in redundancy and conflicting approaches that can lead to waste and an inability to adapt to the needs of the customer, especially in a reasonable period of time. The five Ss (discussed in greater detail in another chapter) are a step toward standardization that enables organizations to operate more efficiently and effectively to deliver a product or service to the customer.

Quality management requires ongoing communication. Communication occurs vertically and horizontally throughout an organization and externally, especially with an external customer. This communication includes both qualitative and quantitative data and information that provide a balanced perspective. Poor communication often results in an inability to determine the effectiveness of change in the level of quality and whether corrective action is necessary.

1.3 DRIVERS FOR LEAN

A number of recent contextual factors have enabled Lean to become a reality (refer to Figure 1.3).

Globalization is perhaps the biggest driver for Lean. Resources from across the globe are assembled to produce a product or deliver a service. Products and services are, in turn, distributed across the globe in a complex supply chain to customers, all with requirements and expectations surrounding price and quality. Lean strives to ensure that the value stream from beginning to end executes smoothly so that customers feel satisfied. Failure to provide the highest quality for the lowest cost can result in a company losing market share, showing a decline in profits, and even failing to survive. Lean focuses on increasing the likelihood of customer satisfaction on a global scale by eliminating waste and addressing customer requirements.

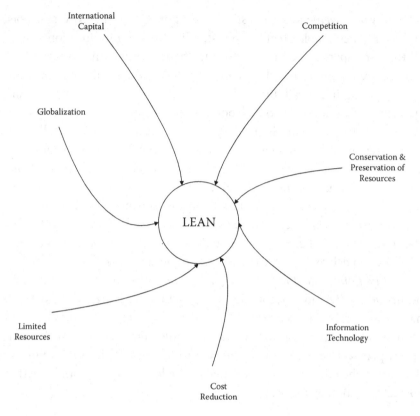

FIGURE 1.3
Drivers for Lean.

Limited resources have become a major concern in recent years. As globalization takes off, the demand for resources will increase dramatically. As the demand increases globally, so does the price. The days of hoarding resources and replenishing them after they spoil, for example, are largely over simply because the cost of the resource will increase and the investment in the existing inventory is lost; such circumstances lead to waste. In addition, inflation increases periodically which, in turn, causes increases in the cost of a product or service being delivered to a customer who in turn, will likely be unhappy about absorbing the cost.

Cost reduction is another related factor. In a global environment, competition is intense simply because there are more competitors that likely can provide the same product or service for the same quality at a cheaper price; competitors can then pass that price advantage to the customer. Waste in all forms puts a company at a disadvantage because until that waste is removed the price will likely be embedded in the product or service to the customer. The customer, in turn, goes to a competitor for the same quality at a cheaper price. Waste in all forms adds to operating costs; a bureaucratic bloated overhead only leads to higher prices to cover costs, which are then passed on to the customer. Lean, of course, helps to reduce or eliminate waste, so that a company remains competitive.

Along with cost reduction is a demand for higher quality products or services. Thanks to globalization, once again competition has become intense and customers expect more for their purchase. As a result, less emphasis is placed on inspection and warranties than on ensuring that quality is being addressed in the processes of building products or providing services. By addressing quality in a process, less need exists for inventory and less overhead is needed for inspections as well as warranty support.

Competition is perhaps the biggest cause for demand for higher quality products or services. Due to globalization, once again, competition can come from any part of the world, not just within the United States. Cheaper products of similar quality will overcome similar products of a higher cost, if the free market is allowed to have its way. The best way to compete, therefore, is to eliminate waste in the value stream so that the cost of a product or service remains competitive relative to other companies across the same industry.

The explosion in information technology serves as a driver, an enabler of processes. Data and information flow freely and quickly unlike in the past. Today, a customer can communicate requirements in a short period of time. A company, such as a manufacturing facility, must respond accordingly if it hopes to retain the customer. If a company continues to rely on legacy systems that impede rather than enhance process performance, the customer may elect to go elsewhere for the product or service. In addition, old systems add to the overhead which creates waste where, in turn, the cost is embedded in the price of the product or service. Lean seeks to improve a value stream by leveraging the power of newer technology, thereby reducing waste associated with cycle time and overhead.

Conservation and preservation of resources is also a driver. Already mentioned is the importance of reducing waste, such as inventory costs. For example, when excessive inventory is held for "just in case" purposes, the items stored in a facility occupy floor space and require some type of oversight to avoid spoilage or pilferage. This situation adds to the overall cost of the product or service, which, after a few significant increases, causes a price increase to the customer. Through conservation and preservation of resources, especially those considered high-cost items, inventory and other wastes can be lowered.

Large investments of international capital have also served as a driver for Lean. Because the value stream may involve resources coming from across the globe, facilities in other countries may require substantial investments. These facilities provide a wide range of resources, subproducts, and expertise often that arrive at a single manufacturing facility. These resources, subproducts, and expertise do not lend themselves to storage due to their demand at other locations or by other competitors. Instead, their delivery must occur based upon pull from the customer, rather than push by the company providing the product or service. Lean stresses the importance of the value stream to flow continuously by eliminating waste, such as holding large inventories.

1.4 LEAN, A LONG HISTORY

Viewing Lean as another flavor of the month would be a grave error. Lean is largely a culmination of quality management concepts, tools, and techniques that have arisen in post–World War II Japan and then, thanks to the Japanese economic challenges to the United States, gained acceptance on the North American continent and eventually around the globe. Thanks to globalization, the need for a more comprehensive approach to address quality arose: Lean focuses on satisfying the requirements of the customer through quality management measures and other disciplines that reduce waste in the value stream.

2

What Is Lean?

Lean is a *customer-focused* approach that concentrates on providing *value* by eliminating waste and increasing quality. It is customer-focused, meaning that a person or organization receives output, such as a product or service, from one or more processes. It provides value by satisfying a customer's requirements. One way to do that is to eliminate waste by removing obstacles that impede the continuous flow of one or more processes delivering output to a customer. In turn, Lean increases quality by reducing defects in the output delivered to the customer.

Therefore, adopting Lean means making the customer the center of attention by capturing a person or organization's specifications, or requirements, and satisfying them using value-added processes, operations, procedures, tools, and techniques deemed worthwhile by the customer. For example, any process or operation that does not satisfy the customer may be considered non-value-added and, consequently, be eliminated. Hence, value-added means those processes, operations, procedures, tools, and techniques that are what the customer is willing to pay for, whereas non-value-added ones do not contribute to what the customer wants. Naturally, it is the latter, non-value-added items, which should be eliminated, that are the fundamental reason for adopting Lean.

2.1 KEY LEAN CONCEPTS

Lean is predicated on several key concepts, shown in Figure 2.1.

Focus on the customer. Under Lean described above, the customer is king. All effort is focused on ensuring that the person or organization meets the requirements of the customer, nothing more and nothing less.

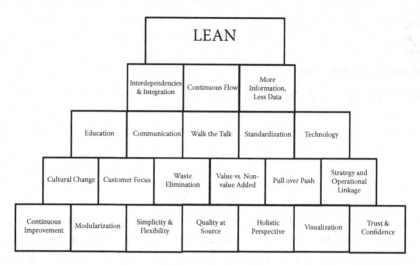

FIGURE 2.1
Key Lean concepts.

The customer becomes the reason for existence of the person or organization. Failure to focus on the customer is, from a Lean perspective, a prescription for failure.

Eliminate waste. Anything that interrupts satisfying customer requirements needs to be removed. Waste not only interferes with satisfying customer requirements; it also adds to operating costs hindering the performance of a person or organization. The concept of waste is referred to as *muda* of which there are two types.

Distinguish between value-added and non-value-added. Processes, operations, procedures, tools, and techniques contributing toward satisfying the requirements of the customer are considered value-added; those not contributing are non-value-added. The non-value-added ones are waste and, therefore, should be eliminated.

Emphasize pull over push. In the not-too-distant past, the emphasis was push rather than pull, meaning that demand was predicated upon past or anticipated requirements of the customer. Pull is the rule today, whereby fulfilling customer requirements is predicated on meeting existing demand. By giving preference to pull, waste such as excessive inventory or overproduction can be more easily eliminated. Of course, pull requires continuous process flow to meet the demand; waste obstructs, interrupts, and sometimes stops, continuous flow.

Stress standardization. Uniqueness is fine, however, when delivering a product or service standardization is critical. Standardization, from a

Lean perspective, applies to processes, operations, procedures, tools, and techniques so that continuous flow can occur; setup times are reduced; and cycle time improves. Through standardization, consistency can occur. Lack of standardization often results in waste, which can interrupt the continuous flow to meet customer demand.

Leverage technology. Although not the center of attention for Lean, technology is seen as an enabler for processes, operations, procedures, tools, and techniques. Under Lean, technology supports executing processes, operations, procedures, tools, and techniques and not the other way around which, unfortunately, is often the case. Technology serves as a means to remove obstacles such as delays in the form of bottlenecks. Technology is also seen as helping people to perform responsibilities when satisfying customer needs, not replacing employees, which again is often the case seen by people in finance.

Stress interdependence and integration. Continuous flow of one or more processes requires that each element within it provide the necessary output to serve as input to the other elements depending upon it, in other words, interdependence. All the elements must also work together as smoothly as possible, in other words, integration. Through interdependence and integration a continuous flow can occur with little or no waste. That, in turn, helps in large part to satisfy customer requirements. The best way to appreciate the concepts of interdependence and integration is to look at the organization as a complex system consisting of objects, or components, that depend upon one another and work together to operate effectively and efficiently. An organization adopting Lean is such a system; anything that interrupts efficiency and effectiveness is waste.

Seek more information, less data. Since the rise of information technology the world has become awash with data, not information. Data are facts that have no intrinsic value; information is data converted into having intrinsic value. The effort in producing and possessing too much data is waste. It is waste because people have to spend time trying to analyze and interpret it. This action can interrupt continuous flow and divert valuable resources that could have focused on satisfying customer requirements. From a Lean perspective, information is king, not data. With information, important decisions can be made more easily and quickly, and waste identified and eliminated.

Seek continuous flow. Lean requires continuous flow based upon the demand of the customer. Ideally, all processes, operations, procedures, tools, and techniques enable continuous flow to meet the requirements of the customer. In reality, of course, no process is perfect and waste that arises interferes with continuous flow. Processes, operations, procedures, tools, and techniques are adapted to differing levels of degree that do not add value. That is often the case for older larger organizations. To ensure that continuous flow occurs and sustains itself, Lean requires the removal of such waste.

Less is more. Redundancy and planned obsolescence are two examples of the opposite of this concept during the days of the push-through system. In the early days, building large stockpiles of parts, for example, was seen as a natural way of doing business to offset shortfalls as well as unanticipated problems with products. Today, the pull-through system is the preferred way of doing business. Through pull, redundancy and stockpiling are done at a minimum or nonexistent level. Pull demand necessitates a continuous flow of a system that provides a product or service that meets customer requirements as they arise. Naturally, more facilities and stockpiling, for example, not only add to costs but also require concentrating on activities that fail to add value.

Modularize. Standardization enables the ability to modularize, meaning to mix and match components of a manual and automated system that supports a value stream. Breaking a system into modules provides greater flexibility in meeting customer requirements by manipulating components or subsets in ways that can reduce waste. For example, certain functionality of a software application may be modified more easily by reducing the impact of a significant change in the configuration. Or, replacing equipment in a work cell can occur more easily if based upon a common standard, thereby reducing setup times. The less a component is based upon a common standard, the more time and labor are required to make a change, adding to setup times that affect cycle time and, ultimately, add to waste.

Seek simplicity and flexibility. Lean seeks simplicity in design by embracing standards and modularization. Complexity leads to waste according to the philosophy of Lean, and it is not hard to understand. Through complexity, adaptation to changing requirements or fixing problems in a value stream can take excessive time and effort to understand. This time and effort to unravel and understand a situation interferes with making timely delivery to the customer by extending cycle time and it does not satisfy pull by the customer. Through standardization and modularization, simplicity becomes possible. Flexibility also becomes possible because it enables participants in a value stream to rearrange the parts, so to speak, to determine the cause of a problem but, just as important, to come up with a solution more quickly and with less effort.

Pursue quality at the source. Under Lean, quality is critical to satisfy the customer. The best way to deliver quality to the customer is to address it at the source, for example, such as during design and development. Traditional ways of dealing with quality, such as through inspections, are not part of Lean. Inspection just before delivering a product or service to a customer is wasteful. It requires overhead in terms of labor and storage of parts, adding to costs that are passed on to the customer. It can also mean slowing down cycle time by clogging the value stream. Not addressing quality at its source can lead to returns and legal complications that not only indicate a degree of dissatisfaction on the part of the customer, but can also hurt the financial bottom line.

Adhere to a holistic perspective. Lean requires a big picture perspective, which is having the ability to look beyond a person's, or organization's, purview. Participants in a value stream see how all the components work together and what impact their responsibilities have on it, as well as upon themselves. By adhering to such a perspective, participants begin to appreciate the importance of their roles and those of others in contributing to customer satisfaction. For example, the failure of a function to perform in a value stream can affect when a product or service is delivered to a customer. Interdependence and integration, mentioned earlier, are significant contributors to the success of a value stream and integral to a successful public or private organization.

Visualize. Graphics have a significant role in Lean in many ways. They are used to capture and improve process flows. They are used to stop production when a problem arises. They are used to reflect progress regarding key performance indicators. They are used to communicate information to various levels of an organization. This visualization is less on displaying data and more on information so decisions and actions can be taken quickly and effectively to ensure the continuous flow of the value streams based upon demand pull, not push. Stoplight charts and scorecards are just two examples of using visualization in Lean.

Link strategy and operations. In many organizations, particularly large ones, strategy sometimes seems disconnected from operations. It seems to create a layer-cake effect whereby the top layer is not aligned with the bottom layer. Under Lean, considerable effort is made to ensure that this situation does not occur. By having everyone up and down the chain of command get into the Lean mind set, and by placing primacy on focusing on satisfying the needs of the customer, both the strategic and operational layers of a company perform as one. Both strategic and operational layers start to adhere to a holistic perspective and seek to reduce waste in daily performance and when delivering a product or service to a customer. Visualization plays a key role in tracking and reporting progress as it relates to tying strategy and operations and encouraging employees at all levels to walk the talk and visit where the action occurs.

Engender trust and confidence. Lean emphasizes trust in the people who do the work by capitalizing on their talents and expertise. That means allowing people to take ownership and come up with ideas to improve process performance in a value stream. Applying this concept, of course, requires management to trust and place confidence in people to do what is right in terms of satisfying the customer through process improvement. It also means management making a commitment not to lay off people as a result of making contributions toward satisfying a customer; to do otherwise will destroy employees' trust and confidence in management. Trust and confidence need to flow up and down the chain of command for Lean to remain a sustaining activity within an organization.

Change the organizational culture. Lean just doesn't happen once executive leadership promulgates it as the new philosophy behind the way of doing business. The groundwork has to be set for Lean to become a reality; that is, more than a flavor of the month program. Lean requires setting the context for it to become a sustaining reality. It is imperative, therefore, that the culture of the organization change; rarely does the culture make it conducive for Lean to have an easy foothold in an organization: trusting subordinates and granting them to take ownership of, not only their immediate responsibilities, but also the operations of the entire enterprise. From an improvement perspective, training people in the concepts and tools of Lean and allowing them the time to engage in improving processes are just some cultural changes that must occur. It largely means that executives and senior management must change from a take-charge, controlling style to one of being supportive and sharing information and even responsibilities with people lower in the organizational hierarchy. In theory that seems innocuous; however, in reality it is harder than what many people think, especially in traditional corporate environments.

Seek perfection through continuous improvement. Lean relies heavily on the concept of continuous improvement. The idea is to seek perfection in everything that is done in the work environment. This pursuit of perfection does not occur in a revolutionary manner but incrementally progresses via an iterative cycle. This pursuit of perfection occurs at all levels of an organization and everything that a person does. The Japanese term, *kaizen*, represents the pursuit of perfection in everything that people do. The focus is actually applying the pursuit of perfection rather than simply talking about it. The PDCA (for plan, do, check, act) cycle, also known as the Deming wheel, is the path to achieve perfection. This wheel repeats itself, rolling its way to a destination, perfection.

Educate people. To implement Lean successfully, people must have the necessary understanding and knowledge about the subject. That means management must invest in education and training, of not only the rank and file but also of themselves. Lean requires a total commitment in providing value to the customer and to do so requires just about everyone to have the necessary knowledge and understanding of Lean concepts, tools, and techniques. People do not change overnight and sometimes require considerable effort to unlearn, as much as learn, about Lean. Over time, people can acquire additional understanding and knowledge through more training and experience as they tackle individual and group projects involving Lean.

Communicate up, down, and laterally. Lean is about people providing people with value. The best way to communicate is more than just pontificating to people about Lean; it requires communication throughout an organization, to and from the machine operator in the corner of a shop floor to the president of the company. This communication goes beyond simply talking to each other about Lean and making proposals for implementation albeit that is also important. It is foremost about listening to others to understand, from a customer perspective, what is of value. It is also about listening to peers to capitalize on their expertise to come up with recommendations for improvement. Communication should be ongoing to further the pursuit of perfection in everything.

Walk the talk. People, from management to the rank and file employee, must live the Lean philosophy. They must perceive, think, and act accordingly. They must become true believers by showing a willingness to learn about Lean, change old habits, and embrace the new ones in their environment. They must also be willing to go where the action is, which includes everyone in the chain of command. That means going out to the customer's environment and learning and observing everything of relevance, and then using that knowledge, changing relevant processes and procedures that will augment value to the customer. By walking the talk, people will also start to make the necessary mind shift to a Lean perspective.

2.2 BENEFITS

Embracing Lean offers many benefits, shown in Figure 2.2.

Understanding customer values. The focus is on the customer, whether an internal or external one. This benefit is really the premier benefit of Lean. By satisfying the customer, all other benefits are realized, too. To realize this benefit requires knowing the needs, wants, and other customer requirements and orienting all processes, procedures, techniques, and so on toward satisfying them. To maximize the payback of this benefit requires considerable effort on the part of the company that delivers the product or service to learn about the customer. It requires people compiling and collecting data and information, interviewing people, conducting extensive reviews of internal and external reports about the customer, and going to the customer's major site locations to observe and learn. Whatever the means, the important point is to know the customer's requirements and then to work to satisfy those deemed important by the customer.

Improving cycle time. The time required to build and deliver a product or service should be in concert with the demand of the customer. The idea is to operate in tandem with the needs of the customer when the customer needs a product or service. Too long or too short a cycle time can frustrate the producer and the customer. It can cause, for instance, a buildup of inventory or a delay in delivering products or services to a customer, both adding waste. Improving the cycle time is a direct benefit of Lean because it improves flow by eliminating waste.

Enhancing shareholder value. Throughout the 1990s, special emphasis was given to delivering shareholders a return on their investment. One key metric was enhancing shareholder value, which was essentially calculated using strategic considerations to provide a solid return to shareholders. Lean is a tool that contributes to shareholder value by reducing waste, such as excessive inventories or delays in delivering a product or service to a customer. Applying Lean concepts, tools, and techniques to a process becomes more efficient and effective, allowing for larger cash flows.

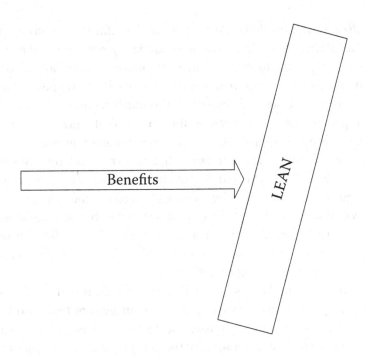

- Understanding of customer values
- Improving cycle time
- Enhancing shareholder value
- Providing greater flexibility
- Providing better quality and reliability
- Reducing capital expenditures
- Reducing organizational hierarchies
- Focusing on core competencies
- Balancing quantitative with the qualitative
- Leveraging technology
- Utilizing resources more efficiently and effectively
- Lessening fear
- Overcoming a silo mentality
- Teaming at greater levels
- Reducing overhead costs
- Engendering an environment conducive to creativity
- Continuously making and tracking improvement

FIGURE 2.2
Lean benefits.

Providing greater flexibility. At first, it may be difficult to envision how Lean can increase flexibility because redundancy sometimes allows for flexibility in response to circumstances. More often than not, however, flexibility is inhibited due to redundancy entrapped in a complex network of supporting processes and resources. Too much redundancy can be as stultifying as too little when responding to an event. Having too much inventory, too many approvals, or a complex process flow are examples that make it difficult to make necessary changes to respond to a customer's dynamic requirements. One particular example is when a simple change in the requirements requested by a customer becomes too costly to a service provider or delays delivery by responding to the change. Lean stresses simplicity through standardization and modularization to allow for rearranging, adding, or deleting components with as little disruption as possible in response to changing conditions.

Providing better quality and reliability. This benefit is realized because Lean involves using a wide range of quality management tools and techniques that focus on reducing waste. Tools such as Pareto and statistical process control charts are just some of the many tools and techniques that can be used to reduce waste and eradicate poor quality as a major focus. Emphasis shifts from building in quality at the source and less on inspecting and keeping inventories for just-in-case scenarios. With quality, of course, comes reliability because the products and services meet customer requirements.

Reducing capital expenditures. Because Lean focuses on reducing wastes in all forms to deliver value to the customer, it makes sense that one of the areas for doing so is in capital expenditures. These expenditures are, for the most part, high-dollar items such as facilities, heavy equipment, and large item storage, to name just a few. Such items require substantial overhead to maintain, house, and keep them in workable order; that translates into costs. Lean works on reducing overhead in an effort to provide value to the customer, which includes a competitive price. It achieves that by adopting a just-in-time delivery of resources, reducing storage space, and decreasing unit costs.

Reducing organizational hierarchies. In many large private and public entities, empire building is common practice. Translated, that means adding more people and greater levels of hierarchy, especially in the executive and management ranks. Naturally, this type of growth has many negative side effects. Communication becomes more difficult; management gets out of touch with what is occurring in the lower-level ranks; negative conflict often erupts as members of executive management compete for greater growth in power and control; and processes become so intertwined that making change is next to impossible because it upsets the power and control of certain people or organizations. In the end, it all translates in a bloated overhead due to salaries, facilities with larger offices and cubicles, and power grabs, all adding to waste. Lean stresses the importance of reducing hierarchies to ensure continuous flow occurs and does not lead to excessive costs affecting the operational efficiency of the company or organization.

Focusing on core competencies. Every organization, private or public, has a set of core competencies, for example, skill sets and expertise, that it performs well. These are strengths. Organizations should concentrate on these strengths as much as possible and enable other organizations to perform the functions or responsibilities that they do better. Outsourcing and just-in-time delivery of goods and services are examples whereby other companies perform work that the recipient organization does not do too well. By focusing on core competencies, an organization can reduce waste and concentrate more on providing value to the customer.

Balancing the qualitative with the quantitative. Many times, value is associated with cost or some other financial metric. Under Lean, cost is but one major consideration to provide value to the customer. Albeit important, cost is often emphasized at the "expense" of the qualitative. Quality, employee morale, and customer relations are just a few examples of qualitative considerations that can add value to a customer and, if not addressed, can add to waste and have a negative impact on quantitative performance. The need for balance between the two is often overlooked and, yet, they have a symbiotic relationship; performance failure in one can affect the other negatively.

Leveraging technology. Technology should serve as an enabler of one or more processes, not the other way around. In many environments, processes are more oriented toward meeting the internal needs of equipment or software applications; the focus shifts to internal requirements rather than those that the customer wants to address. So much effort is made to satisfy the requirements of the machine or application that overhead costs increase and so does cycle time, hence, production does not match customer demand. Ideally, technology should enhance process performance to reduce any waste and allow for continuous flow to provide a product or service to a customer.

Utilizing resources more efficiently and effectively. Bloated overhead due to excessive resources, such as increasing layers of management, is waste.

It does not add value to the customer. It simply increases costs and can interfere with accomplishing goals and objectives concerning customer requirements. Under Lean, the emphasis is on reducing inventories of labor and nonlabor resources. Such reductions in inventories lower production costs but also allow focusing efforts on meeting customer requirements. They improve efficiency and effectiveness with minimal resources by eliminating many examples of waste such as overproduction, dealing with contingencies, or delivering a defective product or service to the customer.

Lessening fear. If Lean is employed as a means for improvement and not to remove people from the workforce, then fear should dissipate. Ideally, and the word here is ideally, no one should lose his or her employment for applying Lean in the work environment. Management should be engendering trust and confidence in employees and granting them the autonomy to take ownership in the work they perform, the processes they support, and support for the entire organization. Employees participating in Lean should not be forced to view it as performing their execution under the pretext of removing waste. Unfortunately, too many times Lean initiatives are conducted resulting in or occurring concurrently with layoffs. Despite management's insistence that Lean and layoffs are unconnected, the perception of a relationship persists. Consequently, trust and confidence decline and Lean becomes a four-letter word.

Overcoming a silo mentality. Lean requires everyone, not just executives, to look at the big picture regarding a company. This perspective is possible because the focus is on customer satisfaction and assurance that a process flows continuously and with minimal waste. Everyone takes ownership in all that happens in an organization, not just what occurs within her functional area of responsibility. In large organizations such a perspective becomes quite difficult, especially if one is deep in the bowels of an organization. Nevertheless, all individuals should know how they contribute toward customer satisfaction by identifying opportunities for waste reduction and improving process flow.

Teaming at greater levels. Although Lean can occur individually or as a group, many improvements occur when people form teams consisting of people from all levels of an organization and from different functional disciplines. Everyone applies the same knowledge, tools, and techniques to improve one or more processes. Each team member provides knowledge and expertise while at the same time looking at the bigger picture as it relates to customer satisfaction. Good communication and team dynamics are critical to a successful Lean project as improvements are identified and implemented within a value stream.

Reducing overhead costs. If waste is removed from a value stream, naturally a reduction of overhead costs should occur accordingly. These reductions can then be transferred to savings for the organization and the customer. These savings can come from many areas, such as storage and transportation. Any reductions in overhead costs should not mean laying people off; doing so will only jeopardize ongoing and future Lean projects.

Engendering an environment conducive to creativity. In some organizations, lip service is paid toward creativity. "Think outside the box" is bandied about when, in reality, doing so may be career limiting. If executive and senior management truly embrace Lean, however, then creativity will become more frequent and pay big dividends by identifying new ways to reduce waste in the value stream, thereby delivering value to the customer. Although not everyone is a creative genius, executive and senior management can provide the necessary support for people to apply creative techniques at the individual and team levels. Additionally, it must allow employees to question the current way of doing business and welcome suggestions for improvement.

Continuously making and tracking improvements. Applying Lean requires identifying and making improvements in an effort to achieve perfection, whether on an individual area of responsibility basis or across a value stream. The idea is that identifying and implementing change also require following up on whether it is effective as intended or pursuing a modified or different course of action. Followup and assessment are continuous until perfection has been, or is close to being, achieved, approaching perfection when waste is removed or reduced and the customer's requirements satisfied.

Transferring and sharing knowledge. With greater trust and confidence, people up and down the chain of command can begin to feel comfortable dealing with topics that address Lean. This feeling of comfort includes a willingness to bring up issues, share insights, and recommend solutions without fear of reprisal. The focus is on satisfying the customer and eliminating waste. People begin to relinquish data and information as well as allow backup of responsibilities, knowing that they will not lose their positions or jobs. Of course, no guarantee of employment exists just about anywhere but to be applied effectively, Lean requires people feeling confident that they can share without negative consequences.

Adapting to changing circumstances. This benefit is very important in today's dynamic business environment. As globalization and market forces expand so does the need for flexibility in responding to changes in the market. If an organization finds itself bloated from waste, it will find itself constrained in its ability to marshal its processes and resources to remain competitive. Lean encourages using standardization, simplicity, modularization, effective resource utilization, modern information technology, and solid communications, to name a few, internally and externally. All are enablers for an organization to adapt to changing circumstances if waste is minimal, perhaps nonexistent.

2.3 CHALLENGES

Despite all the benefits of Lean, trying to make it a reality in an organization can be extremely challenging, as shown in Figure 2.3.

Bureaucracy. Bureaucracy sometimes seems to be a synonym for waste and it can often seem to be the biggest impediment to Lean. This situation especially occurs when first considering Lean. Just the idea of applying Lean can result in people going through myriad approvals and meetings just to recommend looking at the topic. Numerous people will want to get involved in the preliminary discussion and some people may express concern that it might disrupt the current process too much and raise expectations too high. In the end, of course, it is the fear of losing something, such as position or power, which makes bureaucracy so challenging to Lean. After all, in a sense Lean is the antithesis of bureaucracy.

Silos. This challenge is very closely related to bureaucracy. However, it more reflects traditional organizational structure that exists in some organizations. Commonly referred to as stovepipes, each silo represents a discipline, such as information systems or marketing. These stovepipes tend to see a process through their own discipline and protect their power and position vis-à-vis other silos. This structure tends to delay projects and other decisions because each silo contributes its knowledge, expertise, approval, and the like independently of the other silos.

Specialization. From a Lean perspective, specialization can prove a challenge similar to that of a silo. People with very specific knowledge or expertise can delay process improvement activities. The tendency to see a process from their narrow discipline and to use jargon, unless translated,

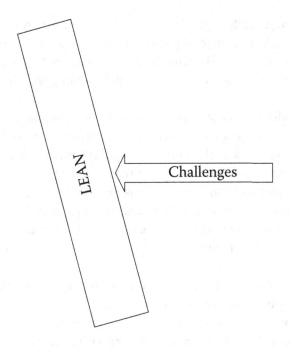

- Bureaucracy
- Silos
- Specialization
- Fear
- Lack of management support
- Past failures
- Inflexible mental models
- Management styles
- Flavor of the month
- Outdated technology
- Lack of available information
- Rapidly changing market conditions
- Lack of Lean expertise
- Traditional accounting practices
- Sacrosanct processes

FIGURE 2.3
Lean challenges.

can cause communication problems. Hence, a designer may view designing as more important than engineers in manufacturing or vice versa. Specialization adds to the challenge by adding complexity in understanding the perspective of each discipline and determining what is and is not important.

Fear. Depending on the state of the economy or an organization, a topic of Lean is often followed by another topic: layoff. Just the word Lean has a connotation of less and that means people will eventually be let go to realize the savings. Unfortunately, Lean receives a bad reputation for this perception. Sometimes, this perception is not too unwarranted, though. Lean sometimes reduces so much waste within a process that people can lose their jobs if no other opportunities exist within their organization. It is this connection to job loss that engenders resistance to Lean although, in fact, they are not related.

Lack of management support. Within every organization, some people will say they embrace Lean and talk it but when it comes to actually doing it, their support is limited or hot air when setting priorities and budgets. In reality, under this circumstance, Lean never had support. Employees who participate in Lean projects know that this support is simply perfunctory and, while working on a Lean project, do so only in a perfunctory manner. This lack of management support is also expressed in other ways, too, besides financial. Political or in-kind support may be tepid or nonexistent from a project sponsor or the topic of Lean is not addressed at significant meetings.

Past failures. Whether for Lean or any other project or initiative, past failure may have likely occurred. These failures will serve as justifications to not perform Lean by claiming it is another boondoggle or flavor of the month. The naysayers will all come out and say that Lean has all the characteristics of a past failure and that good money should be spent elsewhere. Sometimes the correlations have little in common. The assumption is that the past will repeat itself, which has as much relevance and reliability as the assumption that the past will not repeat itself. Each Lean project, like most projects, is unique and the best approach is to learn from the past Leans, successful and unsuccessful ones, and capitalize on the lessons learned.

Inflexible mental models. The mind can become a mental prison, making it very difficult to find an escape. In many organizations, these mental models prevail. They view the environment with a certain lens and interpret everything through it. These models are reinforced through tradition, financial incentives, managerial styles, specialization, and much more. Shattering or questioning these models is tantamount to some people as being iconoclastic. Lean, of course, requires shifting a mindset to come up with innovative ways to remove waste in the value stream and to satisfy the customer.

Management styles. Lean requires an open management style because it requires considerable bravery to ask simple questions such as,"Why?" Some management styles, similar to James McGregor's Theory X approach to management, will likely view such an attitude as equivalent to insurrection or noncompliance when in reality questioning and challenging are core values of Lean. Lean requires warriors, not soldiers. The difference is that warriors focus on the end result and constantly ask themselves and others why things are done a certain way and ask how things can be done better; soldiers simply follow orders by complying with commands. Both are needed, but warriors of Lean embrace the challenge of making Lean a reality.

Flavor of the month. The corporate world is awash with initiatives and programs that declare change is coming for the better. Money, time, and effort are dumped into these initiatives and programs and sold to everyone as lasting ones. Of course, people jump on the bandwagon, take all sorts of training, and attend conferences, for example, only to find a few years later that the people who embraced the change either left or shifted their priorities. Then everyone scurries to join the next flavor of the month, more out of survival for themselves rather than of the organization. Lean is often seen, in some organizations, as another flavor of the month; more often than not, people attend Lean workshops only to find that recommendations for change never get implemented.

Outdated technology. Lean requires looking at technology as an enabler, not an inhibitor of the value stream. Sometimes the technology becomes the focus of attention and everyone works to satisfy its requirements to function. This situation is intensified when legacy systems, that is, old applications, are employed, for example. In many cases, these systems have become so ingrained in the existing process and the investment in maintaining them has become prohibitive; yet, vested interests fight to keep them operating. Change seems almost impossible unless people with a vested interest see a personal gain, rather than a loss, due to system replacement.

Lack of available information. Despite the presence of computing technology, often the information, even the data, to conduct a Lean initiative or project, is unavailable, does not exist, or people do not want to share it.

The former is often lost in a mess of incompatible computing systems or hardcopies stored in a cabinet or back room; the latter is often because of fear in the workplace where the release of information is seen as diluting position or power within an organization. Lean depends on the release of reliable data and information and, without both, a special effort must be made to generate them. Sometimes people see generating data and information about their role in a process or procedure as threatening, such as reflecting poor performance in specific areas of responsibility.

Rapidly changing market conditions. Lean requires at least some time to study the existing value stream. In a dynamic environment, taking the time to capture, for example, the As-Is value stream may render the output irrelevant. That is why it is important to scope a Lean project in a manner that provides sufficient payback while at the same time not taking too long to complete. For large companies, such as a global manufacturing enterprise, making this kind of decision can be quite difficult because of the complexity of the value stream. If the To-Be recommendations are acceptable, too, it can be quite difficult for the same reasons with the added challenge of getting organizations and people to want to change.

Lack of Lean expertise. For a successful Lean project, program, or initiative, people need the necessary knowledge to make meaningful improvements in a value stream. More often than not, however, the necessary knowledge acquisition and transfer come after the fact, that is, once the Lean project, program, or initiative takes place. Naturally, that knowledge comes too late and benefits only subsequent Lean endeavors. Lean is essentially a philosophical approach toward quality, requiring a reorientation from the daily operational mindset that focuses on delivering the product or service without regard to the customer per se. Lean requires putting the customer first with operations squarely focusing on customer satisfaction. Lean expertise, therefore, requires considerable unlearning and relearning.

Traditional accounting practices. Accounting in most corporate environments is based upon generally accepted accounting principles, or GAAP. These principles are intended to provide investors, not necessarily the customer, with reasonable assurance that the company will operate for a considerable time period. GAAP largely requires taking a very functional perspective, that is, a stovepipe perspective of revenue and expenses, thereby long term. This accounting perspective can clash with Lean, which focuses on the value stream, which is often cross-functional and is very project, program, or initiative oriented, thereby short term. The conflict between the two perspectives can hinder Lean when it comes to allocating costs. In some places, an alternative accounting approach is adopted, called activity based costing, or ABC, which allocates costs to specific deliverables produced for a project, program, or initiative.

Sacrosanct processes. In some companies, there is only one acceptable way of business for a value stream. It has been that way for decades and nothing, short of financial devastation, is going to allow making changes to it. The reasons are quite obvious. Vested interests will protect a process else they could face demise in stature within the organization. A process may also be proven so taking a chance by altering or replacing the current way of doing business by entering into the unknown could result in realized risks. Powerful vested interests in the status quo may have a specific reverence for the past. Lean requires questioning on the part of everyone in an organization with emphasis on customer satisfaction. Such questioning is dangerous in an environment replete with sacrosanct processes.

2.4 LEAN AND PROJECT MANAGEMENT

Lean is an approach that, when adopted, provides many benefits. Yet, to realize these benefits requires overcoming many challenges. It is important, therefore, that Lean be applied efficiently and effectively if for no other reason than it requires investing considerable time, money, and effort as well as causing a temporary disruption in providing products and services to the customer. There is only one tool that can help Lean succeed: project management. Without project management, a company will likely not realize the benefits of Lean or overcome the challenges confronting its application.

3

Overview of Project
Management Fundamentals

Before discussing in detail the use of project management (PM) to manage Lean projects, it is important to have a good understanding of what the topic is all about. All too often people talk about PM but fail to understand the fundamentals necessary to make it a reality. Good PM requires knowledge and discipline on the subject. Unfortunately, the overall record of projects completing on time, in just about all industries, is less than satisfactory when measured against three common criteria for success: cost, schedule, and quality. What is covered in this chapter, in concert with the basics of Lean in the next chapter, is a game plan for managing Lean projects.

3.1 WHAT IS A PROJECT?

A project is not something that people do routinely. It addresses something that is unique, that is, never having been done before. If it has been done, then it varies significantly due to unique circumstances, such as requirements being different from previous ones. A project also exists for a finite period of time, varying from a few days to a few years, depending on its scale and complexity. Once a project is complete, the entire effort is disbanded or transferred to ongoing operations (refer to Figure 3.1). Hence, a project is a set of activities or tasks performed in a logical sequence to attain a unique result, for example, a new building or a software application, and then it concludes. All projects also consume resources, which

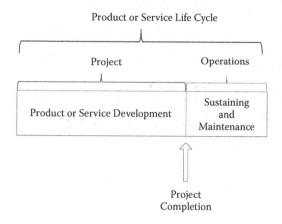

FIGURE 3.1
Project or service life cycle.

include labor, such as people with a specific expertise, and nonlabor, such as time and money.

PM is a discipline to manage projects. It consists of a set of proven concepts, tools, and techniques that enhance the possibility of success, however key stakeholders define it. *Stakeholders* are people or organizations having a direct or indirect interest in the outcome of a project.

PM requires performing these processes: initiating, planning, organizing, executing, monitoring and controlling, and closing. The scale, complexity, and importance of a project will determine the extent to which these processes are addressed. Although not technically a process, there is one that is performed throughout all the other processes, and that is leading. More on that topic later.

3.2 STAKEHOLDERS

As mentioned previously, a stakeholder is a person or organization having a direct or indirect interest in the outcome of a project. The number of stakeholders varies from project to project and from industry to industry. Below is a list of some of the common stakeholders that exist on projects:

- Customers
- Government agencies

- Partners
- Press
- Public at large
- Senior executives
- Shareholders
- Special interest groups
- Suppliers
- Team members
- Users
- Vendors

Often with little or no authority, project managers must also work and communicate with other people involved with their project. They not only have to interact with the team, customer, and steering committee, but they must also act tangentially with a wide category of people in other organizations, including

- Accounting
- Contracts
- Cost engineering
- Employee relations
- Engineering
- Estimating
- Information systems
- Legal
- Operations and maintenance
- Purchasing
- Quality assurance and control
- Records management
- Safety
- Scheduling
- Strategic planning

Stakeholders can play one or more roles on projects. Usually, there are five fundamental roles on a project. These are the sponsor, senior management, customer, project team member, and project manager.

The sponsor is usually a senior manager with single authority to ensure a project is properly supported. The sponsor provides many kinds of support, not all of it financial. He or she can provide political support, resolve issues, and make key decisions. Sometimes the sponsor may be a group of people forming what is known as a steering committee. The project manager may or may not report to the sponsor. Sponsors can be totally involved on a project; or the involvement could be lukewarm at best or it could be nonexistent. Sponsors, too, can change from time to time. Some of the specific responsibilities of a sponsor include organizing and managing the work statement, developing and maintaining relationships with other stakeholders, providing guidance and oversight, making important decisions, and removing key barriers.

Senior management consists of the superiors of the project manager. These are people often in higher management ranks, such as first level or above to all the way up to the C-suite, again depending on the scale, complexity, and visibility of a project. One of the members of senior management usually serves as the sponsor and others attend steering committee meetings. Members of senior management often move around, sometimes making it difficult for the projects to receive stable guidance and support; this situation can be extremely difficult if the sponsor of a project changes too often. Some specific responsibilities of senior management include ensuring their organizations provide the necessary support for the project, making key decisions, and ensuring actions supporting a project align with the goals and objectives of the project.

The customer is the person or organization for which the project is conducted. The customer is, for all practical purposes, the reason for the project in the first place. Whatever the output for the project is, it must eventually go to a customer, whether internally or externally. Defining the customer is not as easy as one would think. For example, a government project that creates a system for use by the public can be a challenge because the public may not be specific enough. It is good to define who or what the customer is for every project, if for no other reason than to understand why a product is being built or service being delivered. Over time, the customer, as well as the requirements, can change. Sometimes, an immediate customer exists but a longer-term one has also been identified. Some of the specific responsibilities of the customer include paying for the product or service being delivered, collaborating with the project manager and the project team, approving interim and final deliverables, providing necessary labor with knowledge and expertise, and defining and communicating requirements.

The project team consists of the people who make it possible to develop a product or deliver a service to the customer. Often, an original core team is established that sets up the initial guidance and plans for the project and then additional members join the team as the project progresses. Some team members support the project full time, whereas others come on board for a short while and then depart. Ideally, a project receives the team members with the requisite skills and knowledge identified in the plan at the right time. Reality, however, may dictate otherwise. In addition, sometimes not all team members perform according to expectations; a common guideline, known as a heuristic, is that 20% of the people produce 80% of the output. The other complication is that turnover of team members on a project is quite common, making it difficult to engender and maintain esprit de corps. Specific responsibilities of the project team include supporting the project manager; applying the requisite skills, knowledge, and expertise; performing as a team; and working with the customer.

The project manager is another major role on a project. This person has overall accountability to complete a project. This is no small responsibility, especially if a project manager has no real authority over team members. It is also a difficult role for the person if she has limited support from the sponsor or senior management. Nonetheless, the project manager is the person held responsible to turn the effort and resources of the project team into a product or service that the customer wants and, therefore, is willing to pay for. The project manager is also the only person who interacts with just about all the other stakeholders. She serves as the hub that all communications funnel through unless, of course, she lacks support from the sponsor or senior management. Some specific responsibilities include establishing effective communication among stakeholders, developing a plan with key stakeholders, ensuring performance according to a performance measurement plan, and motivating the project team.

3.3 PROJECTS, PROGRAMS, PORTFOLIOS

Some organizations, unfortunately too few, apply project portfolio management, a disciplined approach to view projects as an investment to achieve strategic goals and objectives. Each project, program, and initiative is tracked, evaluated, and managed much like an investment in a financial portfolio. Ideally, a project is considered by senior executives as a good investment; otherwise, when budget cuts arrive, it will likely be one of the first victims.

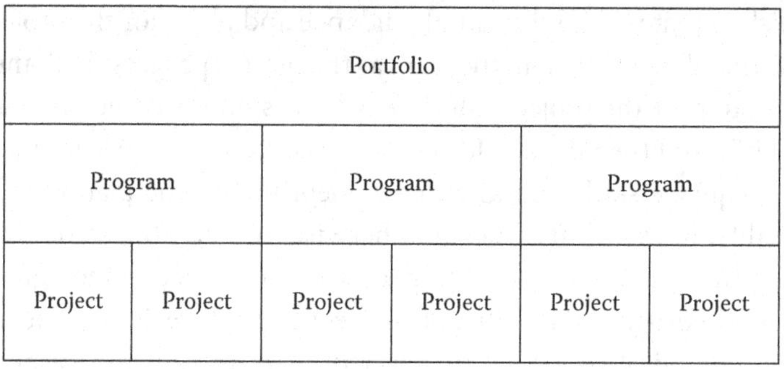

Portfolio					
Program		Program		Program	
Project	Project	Project	Project	Project	Project

FIGURE 3.2
Portfolios, programs, and projects.

A portfolio actually consists of projects, programs, and sometimes initiatives, as shown in Figure 3.2. A program is essentially a group of related projects that satisfy one or more strategic goals and objectives. An initiative often consists of one or more programs or one or more large-scale projects that affect an entire enterprise. Hence, the relationship goes as follows: vision, mission, goals, and objectives; operating plans, initiatives, programs, and projects.

The idea is to ensure all projects, programs, and initiatives add value to the company. If they do not, then they should be scrapped. Portfolio management is the tool to ensure that all three are in alignment with the company. Portfolio management uses wide criteria, often determined by an executive steering committee. The criteria may be financial performance but it may be other variables such as schedule performance, technical performance requirements completion, and burndown of deliverables. Under portfolio management, projects, programs, and initiatives are often put into what are known as strategic buckets, such as strategic, operational, and maintenance. Money and other resources are then apportioned and reapportioned regularly to improve performance of a project, much as with an investment portfolio. In some cases, performance may be so inadequate for a project that it is canceled.

3.4 ORGANIZATIONAL LOCATION OF PROJECTS

Projects can reside in all levels of an organization. The power and visibility of a project depends on its location within a specific structure; it also determines to a large extent how much power and authority a project manager has. There are three fundamental organizational structures where a project may find itself located.

The first is the traditional functional, or stovepipe, organization where a project resides. The company is basically broken into several functional areas, such as marketing, sales, accounting, manufacturing, and engineering. A project may arise in the bowels of one of these functional areas and necessitate the project manager working with a team comprising people from each of the other areas. Obviously, the project manager is going to have little or no control over these people and will need considerable support from his sponsor or senior management to act or make decisions.

The second is the matrix organizational structure. Ideally, the project manager is a member of a PM organization, known as a project management office or PMO, having responsibility to provide PM expertise. Although the people likely report to leadership in a functional area, the project manager has considerable authority to make decisions and to act as they relate to the vision, goals, and objectives of the project. The project manager still needs support from the sponsor and senior management but he can interact with the functional managers regarding the resource. Most of the time, people are supporting multiple projects; sometimes, they are dedicated full time to the project.

The third structure is the projectized or task structure. This structure is the ideal one for a project manager with complete control over resources, labor and nonlabor alike. The project manager has total control over the budget, can negotiate and communicate freely with other stakeholders, and has a dedicated project team. In some cases, a steering team exists to provide some guidance and support, but for the most part the project manager operates the project as an independent business unit.

Realistically, most organizations are a blend of all three structures to one degree or another, especially in medium to large companies. A PM office exists that provides PM expertise, including project manager. Some major projects and programs have their own budget and grant the project manager considerable autonomy. A number of functional organizations, such as finance and information systems, provide resources to the projects and will even have their own internal projects.

3.5 LEADING AND SIX KEY PROCESSES

As shown in Figure 3.3, a project manager performs a very critical action and project management processes on a project. Failure to perform any of them at a satisfactory level can result in performance problems for a project.

Leading is the most important action a project manager can take. It is the only one that applies to all the other actions and project management processes on a project. It entails motivating people to achieve the results of a project. *Leading* is different from *managing*, which is about doing things right; leading is about doing the right things. For example, PM is about performing the functions such as scheduling, calculating costs, and implementing change management; leading is about working with all kinds of stakeholders, applying effective listening, resolving conflict, raising issues, and other "soft" topics related to intra- and interpersonal skills. There are many types of leadership styles that can be exercised on a project. These range from being autocratic to taking a laissez-faire orientation.

Although the project manager must lead on a full-time basis, in actuality everyone on a project exhibits leadership to one degree or another. Leading entails communicating with and influencing a wide range of

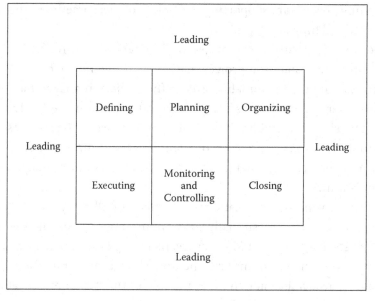

FIGURE 3.3
Leading and project management processes.

stakeholders, confronting issues and problems up front, making timely decisions, collaborating with all stakeholders, and reporting all results, including the good and bad. Ultimately, there is no specific deliverable produced from leading but all deliverables for a project and the final product or service that reflects the quality of leadership exhibited on a project. Leading is instrumental in ensuring that the following project management processes are implemented effectively on any project.

Defining is determining in advance what a project will achieve. This process is extremely important because it essentially formulates the entire purpose of the project. Defining entails drafting a charter, preparing a statement of work, determining requirements, and obtaining buy-in from key stakeholders. The most significant deliverable from defining is the project charter and the statement of work. Both deliverables provide a high-level vision for the project that serves as a basis for performing all subsequent actions and determining success once the project completes.

Planning is determining what activities or tasks are needed to execute the vision of the project, assigning who will perform those activities, and identifying when those activities must start and stop. This process is quite extensive and much effort should be put into it because it serves as a road map for realizing the vision for the project. Actions to perform include defining the scope in greater detail, determining a schedule to complete the work, assigning people to perform the activities, calculating financial requirements, and identifying risks and ways to respond to them. There is a wide range of deliverables produced as a result of this action. These deliverables include a work breakdown structure (WBS), a network diagram, schedules, time and cost estimates, allocating and assigning resources, creating a budget, and performing risk management. Once all these deliverables are produced and bought off by key stakeholders, a performance measurement baseline is established for three areas: cost, schedule, and scope. The performance measurement baseline is used to manage a project and to evaluate its performance. Keep in mind that there is an agreement between two or more stakeholders on expectations about the performance of a project.

Organizing is employing resources efficiently and effectively to manage a project. This action involves establishing the infrastructure for managing a project. It involves activities such as determining tools, documentation requirements, and organizational structure. Some deliverables for this action include a communication management plan, status reports, hardcopy or electronic forms, organization chart, and roles, responsibilities, and authorities. A management plan is often produced to describe how the project will be conducted; depending on the size of the project, it could be one plan or subdivided into multiple management plans.

Executing is the process involving implementing a plan for the project to achieve its goals and objectives. In other words, it involves managing according to the performance measurement baseline that was built under planning. A key activity under this action is change management, which is the policies, processes, and procedures established on a project to detect, analyze, evaluate, and implement changes to all baselines. These changes can be technical or business in nature. Changes can come from many sources, including the project manager, senior management, customer, project team, or an external entity, such as the government. Successful execution depends on controlling the scope by avoiding what is known as scope creep. If unauthorized changes are made to the original scope, then expectations surrounding the performance measurement baseline will be dashed and no matter how good the quality of the deliverables the customer could be dissatisfied. Some significant deliverables produced during this action include a change control log, applying change and configuration management disciplines, revisiting the performance measurement baseline to determine the impact of a change, and closely performing in concert with the following process, monitoring and controlling.

Monitoring and controlling involves assessing how well a project uses its plan and organization to meet its goals and objectives. Some activities include tracking and monitoring performance, collecting and assessing status, and taking an appropriate response. When collecting status keep in mind two important behaviors, persistency and consistency. Being persistent means collecting status from people and organizations without exception. Many times people will resist giving status out of lack of time but mostly out of fear. Seasoned project managers recognize this aspect of human behavior and, it is hoped, deal with it in a positive manner but do not refrain totally from employing a negative approach. They are also consistent in the collection of data and information, avoiding the tendency to take different approaches with different people, with inconsistent results; the assessment ends up comparing apples to oranges. Assuming no problems with persistency and consistency, a key result from monitoring and controlling is variance. Not all projects perform according to their performance measurement baselines; in fact, most do not. The status output will likely show what is known as *variance*, the difference between what was planned and what actually occurred. If the variance is significant, then the question is whether the variance is negative. If so, what type of corrective action is required or is it even warranted? Is corrective action enough? Could it involve replanning a portion or all of a project?

Closing is the final process. It involves concluding a project efficiently and effectively. Some activities for this process include compiling data and information, conducting reviews, and obtaining buyoffs. Some of the major deliverables for this project are records compilation, financial close-out, contract compliance verification, product verification and validation, process audits, and lessons learned. Quite often, this process is left incomplete on many projects, which is bad because the data and information can avoid legal complications as well as enable project managers of future projects of a similar nature to leverage knowledge and experience from the current one. Some reasons why closing is often neglected are that people who just want to retire from the project, especially if it is a difficult, long, drawn-out affair, are anxious to move on to the next project, and simply because it requires seeking and compiling data and information.

3.6 PROJECT PHASES AND PROJECT MANAGEMENT PROCESSES

A project consists of phases as opposed to processes (refer to Figure 3.4). *Processes* are what the project manager performs, such as leading, defining, and executing; *phases* are discrete periods within a life cycle that require producing a unique set of deliverables, such as a requirements document or software code. Project managers apply the seven processes within each phase and for the overall project.

Consider the following generic example of a project. Call it Project A, which has a mission to develop an accounting system. The life cycle of Project A has four phases: define, design, develop, and deploy. The define phase requires identifying and documenting the requirements; design, building the overall architecture of the accounting system; develop, turning the architectural design into something tangible, such as a software code; and deploy, testing the components and deploying the system into the customer's environment. These phases can occur concurrently or sequentially, depending on the methodology used to build the accounting system. For purposes of understanding, assume that all phases occur sequentially; that is, one phase completes and then the next one can begin.

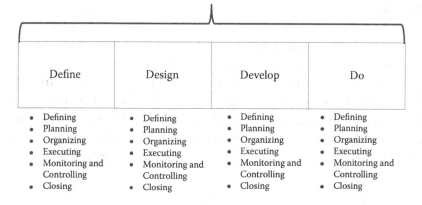

Project Management

- Defining
- Planning
- Organizing
- Executing
- Monitoring and Controlling
- Closing

Define	Design	Develop	Do

- Defining
- Planning
- Organizing
- Executing
- Monitoring and Controlling
- Closing

- Defining
- Planning
- Organizing
- Executing
- Monitoring and Controlling
- Closing

- Defining
- Planning
- Organizing
- Executing
- Monitoring and Controlling
- Closing

- Defining
- Planning
- Organizing
- Executing
- Monitoring and Controlling
- Closing

FIGURE 3.4
Generic phases of a project and project management processes.

The project manager applies the PM processes for the overall project. She leads by taking the initiative to identify all the key stakeholders with the help of the project sponsor. If not developed yet, the project manager drafts the charter and, with the approval of the sponsor, solicits the input from important stakeholders and prepares the document. If the project manager must draft the charter, she will ideally have some prior information, such as a business case, memoranda, reports, studies, and lessons learned to prepare the draft. If not, then the project manager will have to rely totally on input from the stakeholders. The project manager then facilitates, unless the sponsor elects to do so, one or more sessions to come up with a charter.

With the charter complete, the project manager has a core group of people assigned to her to help develop the plans for the project. These plans, depending on the scale, complexity, and visibility of the project, serve as the basis for managing a project. The core team should start, using the charter, to develop a WBS, which serves as the scope for the project but also as a means to develop cost and schedule plans, too.

With the WBS complete, the project manager works with the core team and other stakeholders deemed interested in the project to determine time estimates for each of the activities identified in the lowest level of the WBS. The time estimates are preliminary at this stage and a host of different approaches may be used to make the estimates. The project manager and the core team also determine the resources requirements, which will help to determine the people with the requisite knowledge, expertise, experience, and quantity to perform each activity. In some cases, the project manager and the core team may determine nonlabor needs to perform an activity.

After identifying time estimates and resource requirements, the project manager and the core team can begin to construct a schedule. Again, remember that all this work is still preliminary. The project manager and core team take the lowest-level activities identified in the WBS and logically tie them together, forming a network diagram. Then they apply the estimates to the activities, converting the estimates into durations. Next, they calculate the early start and finish dates followed by the late start and finish dates. The calculation then reveals what is known as the critical path, that is, the activities that cannot slide or there will be a subsequent impact on the critical path. The project manager and the core team will likely have to make several alterations to the schedule to ensure that the work to complete is practical within the time available for completion. The detail schedule provides the basis to develop what are known as a roll-up, or summary, schedule, such as bar charts and milestone charts.

It is at this point in time that costs are prepared for the project. These costs include both labor and nonlabor resources as well as any overhead costs, such as ones related to facilities and training, being apportioned among activities in the project. The costs will determine the budget for the project.

Another important planning exercise for the project is determining the risks. (A *risk* is something that potentially can occur in the future; an *issue* is something that already exists.) The project manager and the core team hold a session to conduct risk management. This exercise involves identifying risks, determining their likelihood or probability of occurrence and their impacts, and the potential strategies and actions to take if a risk occurs. Risk management is visited from time to time on the project to determine its validity and reliability under changing circumstances.

Still another important planning output is the communication management plan. The communication management plan enables providing the right information to the right people or organizations at the right time in the right amount. The first prerequisite for putting together a communication management plan is, of course, to identify the primary stakeholders on the project. Using that information the project manager identifies who needs what information and how much, when, where, and why. This plan is often captured in a matrix and is updated periodically because stakeholders and their requirements change from time to time.

With the cost, schedule, and scope defined for the project in the charter, the project manager can now present the plans to the project sponsor or a steering committee to receive buy-in prior to beginning work.

If the sponsor or steering committee approves the plan, the project manager can then, barring no major revisions, create three baselines: one for the scope, one for the costs, and one for the schedule. Any changes to any of them could have a significant impact on the other; therefore, it is important to have all three under configuration management and any changes should proceed through change management prior to implementation.

As the planning comes to completion the project manager along with the project sponsor may start procuring the necessary labor and nonlabor resources. This effort will ensure that the request for people, equipment, supplies, and so on satisfies any lead time requirements to procuring resources before relevant activities start. The lack of available resources can cause a serious delay in progress. These lead times should appear in the schedule to ensure visibility of their impact should the resources fail to arrive on time.

Often occurring concurrently with the planning process during the define phase of the project is putting together a supporting infrastructure that was discussed earlier about the organizing process. During this period, the project manager, in concert with the core team and selected stakeholders, lays the groundwork to manage the project. The deliverables created at this point in time in the life cycle include creating formats for reports and forms to manage the project; preparing an organization chart; defining roles, responsibilities, and authorities; selecting software tools; and preparing one or more documents describing some of the administrative processes for managing a project. Some topics discussed in these documents include configuration management, change management, risk management, scheduling, reporting, quality management, personnel management, procurement management, and communication management. Depending on the scale, complexity, and visibility of the project, these documents can be created as one entire plan with each one being a separate document.

During the design, develop, and deploy phases of the project, the same PM processes may be applied but usually from a revision perspective. All PM deliverables and processes are subject to revision by applying change management. Rarely does a project occur according to plan; circumstances change and problems are uncovered by the team or the customer. However, any change needs to be controlled to ensure that scope creep, the gradual unauthorized expansion of what is expected by the customer, does not become a reality. Scope creep can wreak havoc on a project, eating away at the schedule and budget while simultaneously causing expansion of the scope. The key is to manage change and not let change manage you. The executing process becomes, therefore, the most critical one during the remaining phases.

Many reasons exist as to why people want to circumvent change management. They may want to please the customer. They may not want to wade through the administrative process often associated with change management. They may want to get an unpleasant activity out of the way and make changes without dealing with anyone. Whatever the reason, project managers must insist on using change management to ensure the integrity of the product or service being delivered to the customer and to preserve the performance measurement baseline for accurate reporting.

During the remaining phases, the project manager during the executing process performs monitoring and controlling. This action requires collecting data and information about the technical and business performance of the project. Data and information are used to assess and evaluate performance and then decide to proceed with the status quo, take corrective action, or replan. When collecting data and information, the data and information should be scrubbed for validity and reliability and then used to generate a series of reports regarding performance. These reports usually are identified in the communication management plan and are distributed accordingly.

The closing process is also important. One of the most important deliverables is creating a lessons learned document. This document provides essential information about what went well during the project and the areas needing improvement. It also captures information on recommendations for improvement. The lessons learned document serves many purposes, but two significant ones are that it serves as a debriefing opportunity among stakeholders and that it provides valuable information about the project to stakeholders of future projects of a similar nature. The project managers of future projects can capitalize on what went well and leverage this information and data to avoid problems and overcome challenges. Lessons learned documents can be developed during the end of each phase and compiled at the end. This approach works best for large, lengthy, complex projects because explicit and tacit knowledge contributing to the content of the document may be lost due to forgetfulness by stakeholders or turnover of people.

Of course, closing involves more than preparing a lessons learned document. It also includes concluding contracts, shoring up financial obligations, and archiving data and information. This action is often overlooked because many people are glad the project is complete; it seems anticlimatic; and has a bureaucratic flavor to it. Yet, closing is very important because it helps avoid or prepare for legal complications, eases the effort and pain associated with audits, and provides a useful database for future projects. As with the lessons learned document, these actions can occur during the end of each phase as well as at the end of the project.

3.7 HOW MUCH PROJECT MANAGEMENT IS ENOUGH?

Unfortunately, a judgment call is required to answer the above question and it is not solely made by the project manager. He works with the participation of the stakeholders including the sponsor and the team to help make that decision. However, there are some heuristics, or rules of thumb, to consider when making this decision.

Maturity in PM is one heuristic. Have stakeholders had the necessary training and experience to understand the purposes and under what circumstances to use the tools and techniques of PM? Usually the less knowledge and experience of PM, the more difficult it becomes to manage large complex projects. Smaller projects, depending how that is defined within organizations, may require what has been euphemistically defined as *PM lite*, whereby the requirements for applying PM concepts, tools, and techniques are less robust than for larger ones.

The existence of a PM framework or methodology coupled with supporting processes and systems within an organization is a heuristic. Usually mature organizations have some framework or methodology to manage projects; ones not as mature will likely operate in a less formal manner. If a framework or methodology is available, then use it. If none exists, PM will often be necessary to instill confidence among stakeholders in the project team. However, keep in mind that more is not necessarily better. Too much PM can cause pushback from some stakeholders and will likely require management support. In some environments, project management is viewed as an inhibitor to creativity and productivity. The key is to tailor the concepts, tools, and techniques to the environment.

The visibility of a project is another important heuristic. Regardless of size or complexity, formal PM disciplines are often preferable over less formal ones. The reasons are that executive leadership will have a greater confidence in knowing how well the project is going and will feel more comfortable in the status information they receive. The biggest challenge in this respect is that some executives may find PM too bureaucratic due to a lack of understanding of the topic. They may agree with comments such as the PM is interfering with the "real work" to get done. The danger is that if such an attitude prevails and the project does not meet expectations, the project manager is usually held responsible.

Again, if a project manager and the team have to determine the degree of PM, it is best to err on more, not less, and formal, not informal, application. Then through trial and error review with stakeholders the degree of application can be adjusted to a scale more suitable to the stakeholders.

3.8 ENTERPRISE PROJECT MANAGEMENT

In recent years, public and private organizations have seen the value of applying PM on individual projects of all scales. Increasingly, these organizations have looked at applying PM not on a project-by-project basis but organization-wide. Enterprise project management, or EPM, is the means to do just that.

EPM requires taking a macro view of an enterprise by requiring projects to follow a systematic approach toward ensuring that projects use a common set of tools and techniques, for example, rather than each project operating on its own and being eclectic in application. Some elements of EPM include ensuring that all projects have some business justification, such as furthering the strategic goals of the organization, following a standard approach and toolset and techniques, enhancing employee knowledge and education of the discipline, seeking continuous improvement in applying PM and sharing best practices, and encouraging and sustaining communication among stakeholders.

If a project is large enough, perhaps even at the scale of a program, then it may have a project management office, or PMO. This office supports the project manager by providing PM expertise with a variety of tools and techniques. A PMO is usually staffed with people having experience and expertise in project management and who possess a holistic perspective about the project and PM. The PMO can concentrate solely on one, more, or all of these activities: collecting and reporting status; providing tools and templates; training people; sharing project management expertise; identifying and communicating about best practices; defining roles, responsibilities, and authorities; and applying efficient and effective resource utilization. Depending on the scale of a project, a small one may simply include a PM assistant and a scheduler. On large projects and programs, a PMO may have a staff of five to seven people who include one or more PM assistants, schedulers, facilitators, and project managers. At the more strategic level of an organization, a PMO can exist that provides many services at a high level. Then other project PMOs can cascade that knowledge and expertise down to their respective projects.

3.9 PROJECT MANAGEMENT IS NECESSARY

PM is absolutely critical to the success of Lean projects. Lean projects suffer from many of the similar problems, challenges, and risks on other kinds of projects when PM is not applied effectively or not applied at all. It is imperative for any project, regardless of industry, to apply the discipline of PM to their Lean projects if they hope to improve their value streams and satisfy customers efficiently and effectively. To achieve that, a project manager needs to exercise the fundamental actions described above for the overall project and within each phase. In some cases, project managers may have to determine and tailor PM on their projects, whereas others may simply follow a standard set of practices identified by a PMO at the project or even enterprise level.

4

Fundamental Lean Concepts, Tools, and Techniques

Although project managers (PMs) do not have to be Lean experts, they should be familiar with the concepts, tools, and techniques for managing and leading a Lean project, shown in Figure 4.1.

For ease of understanding, the material is presented in this sequence:

- Determine Context
- Capture Existing and Proposed Value Streams
- Define Requirements
- Collect Data and Information
- Perform Analysis
- Apply Tools and Techniques for Solutions
- Make Recommendations
- Plan and Execute for Results

4.1 DETERMINE CONTEXT

Project managers have many responsibilities. One of these responsibilities is to understand the environment in which their projects will occur.

There are essentially two types of environments in which Lean projects occur. One environment is known as brownfield, whereby the Lean project or projects will seek to transform an existing facility or organization that employs mass-productionlike processes, methods, and techniques. It is essentially the typical traditional stovepipe environment with characteristics such as being bureaucratic, anticipating customer needs, and

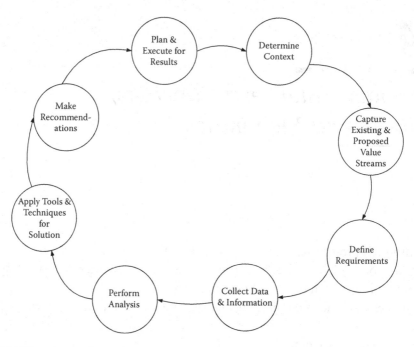

FIGURE 4.1
General concepts, tools, and techniques for using Lean.

stocking inventories. The other environment is creating a new facility or organization employing best practices, methods, and techniques. This environment, known as greenfield, seeks to eliminate the shortcomings and excessive overhead of the brownfield environment.

Most project managers rarely have the opportunity to manage a Lean project in a greenfield environment; instead, their experience is mainly in the brownfield. To some extent, the brownfield environment is more difficult for several reasons. The project managers must challenge the status quo, thereby potentially generating resistance from those people or organizations having something to lose. It also takes a brownfield project a much longer time to complete to resolve political differences and obtain approvals for any significant change. The challenge to the greenfield environment is also fear but for different reasons. One reason is the dearth of knowledge and expertise by people who must institute new processes, methods, and techniques. The other is fear of failure. A new facility or organization must demonstrate its worth in satisfying the customers, especially if the greenfield promises to outperform the brownfield environment. Some stakeholders in the brownfield environment may wait for the greenfield to fail.

In this book, the emphasis is on applying project management (PM) on Lean projects in the brownfield environments.

Selecting a project to apply Lean must be tied to the strategic goals and objectives of a parent organization. In other words, the strategic and tactical operations must link with one another and operate in concert; otherwise, as mentioned earlier in the PM chapter, a layer-cake effect exists, whereby the top layer and the bottom layer are askew, as shown in Figure 4.2.

Lean adopts what is known as the Hoshin Kanri planning system, whereby a systematic approach for decision-making at the strategic and tactical levels aligns them with each other to achieve business objectives. The whole idea is to ensure alignment with the long- and short-strategic and tactical behavior by identifying strategic goals and objectives with the latter being measurable, developing tactical objectives to achieve the goals and objectives, measuring progress toward achieving both strategic and tactical objectives, creating a series of tables to review progress on a regular basis among different levels within an organization, and applying a continuous improvement perspective.

Hoshin Kanri is predicated on numeric performance, specifically financial. Not everything occurring in an organization is measurable from a financial perspective. Quite frankly, it is often more the nonfinancial aspects that make or break a project, program, or initiative, regardless of project, whether Lean or non-Lean. Many companies track performance using what is known as a balanced scorecard. The balanced scorecard is a way to offset the devastating effects of relying solely on financial metrics. Its purpose is to look at the strategic performance from different perspectives, frequently using four variables: financial, customer, internal

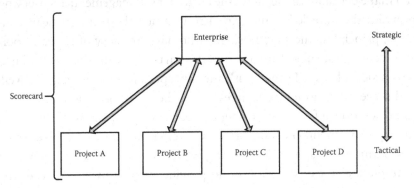

FIGURE 4.2
Strategic alignment of Lean projects.

business process, and learning and growth. For each category, measures are developed that enable tracking performance in the four areas albeit in some organizations a different set of variables may exist.

One advantage of a balanced scorecard is that it provides a holistic perspective as opposed to a narrow financial one. Another advantage is that it demonstrates the need to apply measurable criteria to track other areas of interest. Like Hoshin Kanri, a balanced scorecard should be reviewed periodically after measurements have been taken and followup conducted on the results.

Armed with information from Hoshin Kanri and the balanced scorecard, project managers of Lean projects have a good idea how to posture their Lean projects to fulfill the strategic goals and objectives of the parent organization. In many cases, a business case may be developed to determine if a project is warranted and, if so, the project becomes part of a portfolio of projects. The business case should reference in its justifications the contents of the Hoshin Kanri and balanced scorecard efforts. The business case is then reviewed periodically against the performance of the project to ascertain the realization of benefits and whether corrective action is necessary.

The next action is to formulate a well-balanced team with the requisite knowledge, background, and expertise. This team consists of a core membership for the Lean project, meaning the strategic and tactical decisions are made by this group. It consists of a project manager who has overall responsibility for the leadership and management of the Lean project; a customer representative, the person or organization benefiting from the Lean project, who has the requisite knowledge of their business and who can make decisions on behalf of the customer's management; a sensei who provides the knowledge and expertise to guide the team on Lean concepts, principles, and practices, and who has a mastery of relevant tools and techniques; subject matter experts, particularly on the overall business process being "Leaned out" and any specialized knowledge as well, and serve as authoritative sources for guidance, information, and problem resolution; a facilitator to conduct team meetings and workshops and to help team members collaborate in an environment that enables open communications and builds trusting relationships; on occasion, a project champion, also called a sponsor, to provide support by setting and sustaining the direction and momentum through a project's life cycle; and any other stakeholder deemed essential to the success of the project.

The actual identification of the team members, especially core team members, at this time, is done by conducting a stakeholder analysis. This analysis, of course, depends on the scope of the process being Leaned out. The selection of certain stakeholders on the core team should likely be done with the input and guidance of the project champion and, sometimes, with the direction of a steering committee. Regardless, stakeholder analysis should seek to identify and analyze the individuals and organizations that participate in the current process, or value stream, and any future ones. Later in this book, the challenges of identifying stakeholders are discussed.

A Lean project basically seeks to remove waste in an effort to achieve one overriding goal: customer satisfaction. Admittedly, the term customer satisfaction is an ambiguous term that often leads to disagreements, conflicts, and disappointments. Lean hopes to deal with this ambiguity by insisting on meeting the expectations surrounding customer satisfaction by meeting some subsidiary goals.

One subsidiary goal is to identify and address requirements and expectations of the customer through communication based upon pull rather than push. *Pull* is the movement of resources from the end of a process, or value stream, for example, delivery to the customer, to the beginning of the value stream, for example, request or order, upon receiving some type of signal to deliver a product or service. *Push* is the movement of resources from the beginning of the value stream, for example, design, to the end of the value stream, for example, delivery based upon forecasting a customer's need for a product or service.

A second subsidiary goal is to remove waste that may interfere with pull. Waste consists of operations, activities, resources, and the like that generate output that provides no value to the customer, also referred to as non-value-added. Waste interferes with pull by the customer and adds to inefficiencies, which is wasteful. No waste is considered sacrosanct; if it fails to add value it is targeted for potential removal.

A third subsidiary goal is, therefore, is to seek perfection, which is eliminating waste. By striving for perfection, the process, or value stream, is based upon pull by the customer. Waste is what interferes with this pull. A process is one step closer to perfection when waste is removed.

A fourth subsidiary goal is to achieve continuous flow, which is the ongoing uninterrupted execution of a process. Under continuous flow, pull, not push, reigns because stoppages, scrap, and other waste are virtually nonexistent, especially if perfection is achieved. The lack of continuous flow is due to waste, which is not a state of perfection according to Lean.

For a Lean project to succeed in achieving those subsidiary goals, and the ultimate goal of customer satisfaction, the following conditions must exist just to allow the team to work effectively. Theoretically, these conditions make sense; realistically, they often pose a significant challenge.

Open book management is one condition. All information, and especially managerial in nature related to a process, should be available to all employees who seek to provide value to a customer. Just about all information, including proprietary or competition-sensitive information, must be available, which, quite honestly, often makes management nervous. If Lean is to achieve its goal, however, people require open book management. Think for a moment. If people try to improve a process, especially a complex one, and are not allowed access to data and information that they need to remove waste, they must operate on assumptions. Assumptions are treated as true until proven otherwise. The challenge arises when some people base their thinking on erroneous assumptions without realizing it. If they have actual facts, data, and information on hand then they can debunk certain assumptions. As Alan Mullaly, a top executive formerly with Boeing and Ford says, the data will set you free.

Gemba is another condition that must exist for Lean projects to succeed. Gemba is visiting the location where the work is actually being performed. Through visitation, people will better understand the work of the customer and how to add or increase value to the customer. People on Lean projects need to know and understand the customer's needs and wants to agree to or come up with recommendations for improvement. It pays for some people on Lean projects to step away from their computer screens as well as their cubicles and offices and to go periodically where the action is, whether inside the company or at the customer's site. This concept is related to the managerial concept of management by walking around (MBWA), whereby people visit places to see what is happening and do not just compile data in an electronic file. Visiting the place of action enables seeing exactly what is occurring, taking note of what is and is not working, and obtaining reliable data and information about process performance. This set of actions is known as three (3) gen in Lean parlance. By the way, practicing gemba is another excellent way to debunk assumptions.

Known as quality functional deployment (QFD) in Lean-speak, this condition involves establishing a multidisciplinary team that focuses on customer expectations and needs to ensure the value stream satisfies the customer. This multidisciplinary team offsets a host of problems that often plague teams, including functional myopia and groupthink. By establishing a multidisciplinary team a holistic perspective is possible, offsetting these problems. Multidisciplinary teams also get people engaged early on through discussions, as well as eliminate many misunderstandings. Such teams also help them to get a better understanding of the big picture and to see how their area of responsibility and those of others fit within the value stream.

A final condition for effective Lean projects is to establish tollgates, which are also referred to as stage gates or check point reviews. Tollgates are meetings held at specific phases of a Lean project life cycle to determine progress to date and to decide whether to proceed from one phase to the next. Tollgates serve as a sort of timeout to determine what has been done to date and whether the time is right to proceed forward. In a sense, it is quality control for the Lean project. Tollgates reduce the chance of oversights that can result from making decisions endangering project success.

There are several approaches toward Lean projects, depending on the extent of change that will affect a value stream. Keep in mind that the purpose of Lean is to focus on the customer by providing value through eliminating waste while simultaneously increasing quality.

There are two fundamental orientations to pursue Lean in an existing, or brownfield, organization. The first orientation is to transform the organization radically with a complete set of processes. Lean has a term for this orientation, called kaikaku. It is the radical version of Lean, whereby breakthrough changes are identified and implemented with speed and impact over a short timeframe. The changes are essentially wholesale rather than incremental.

The opposite side of the spectrum is kaizen. Changes are implemented incrementally. Radical change, if it does come, is with less intensity and impact than kaikaku. The pursuit of perfection occurs in small steps until waste is removed from the process. This book focuses on kaizen, not kaikaku.

Kaizen can be executed using one of two structures, or life cycles. The first is using the PDCA cycle and the other, DMAIC, as shown in Figure 4.3.

PDCA stands for plan, do, check, act. These are the four phases of the cycle, with plan involving determining the problem or issue; do is developing and implementing a solution; check is for determining the effectiveness of the solution and making necessary changes; and act is for taking corrective action. The entire cycle repeats itself until perfection has been reached.

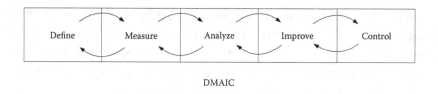

DMAIC

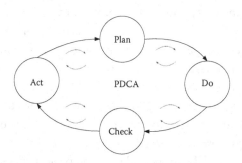

FIGURE 4.3
Two basic Lean life cycles.

DMAIC stands for define, measure, analyze, improve, and control. Define involves determining exactly the problem or goal, measure for establishing metrics and a baseline for performance, analyze for identifying and validating the root cause, improve for testing and implementing the solution, and control for monitoring the effectiveness of the improvement and exercising change management.

Both life cycles work. The original differences between the two are that PDCA is less mathematical in nature and DMAIC relies more on calculations. DMAIC is associated with Six Sigma, which is employed at Motorola. Over time, either PDCA or DMAIC can be applied on Lean, with or without the emphasis on statistical methods. This book uses both the PDCA and DMAIC life cycles.

4.2 CAPTURE EXISTING AND PROPOSED VALUE STREAMS

Whether using the PDCA cycle or DMAIC, it is important to know something about the current process and, employing the PDCA or DMAIC life cycle, to have some idea of the new one that will be the result. The current process is commonly referred to as a value stream, consisting of operations and activities of a process, such as placing an order, to the completion of a process, such as delivery to the customer. The value stream may be more comprehensive, reflecting all operations, procedures, and activities, value and non-value-added, from the point of extracting raw material, such as data or minerals, to the delivery of the product or service to the customer.

The value stream is reflected in maps. These maps make understandability relatively easy in comparison with other ways to display information. Waste is often hard to detect because it is invisible to most people and difficult to articulate to others. Many people lack the jargon or knowledge of process improvement or they have difficulty in seeing and assessing the big picture due to the narrow specialty of their work or their position in the organization. With the help of a map, replete with symbols and specific data and information, people can overcome such limitations and can provide insights as an individual or team member to help remove waste (refer to Figure 4.4).

Three maps, generically referred to as a group as value stream maps, graphically display the routing of materials, information, and other resources through the operations and activities of a process up to the delivery of a product or service to the customer. The three maps are current state value stream map, future state value stream map, and ideal state value stream map. Figure 4.5 is an example of a generic value stream map.

The current state value stream map displays the sequence and interaction of elements of a process that currently exists. It is often referred as the To-Be map.

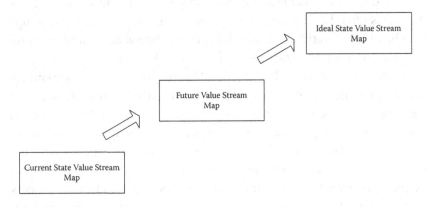

FIGURE 4.4
Value stream maps.

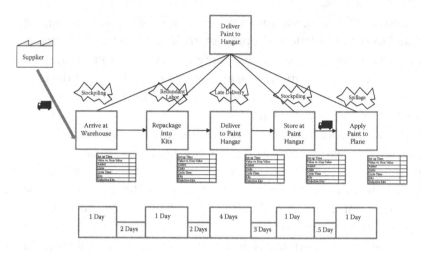

FIGURE 4.5
Generic value stream map (example).

The future state value stream map depicts a process in an improved state, serving as a stepping-stone to a perfect state where continuous flow exists. The ideal state value stream map depicts a process in a perfect state, providing only value-added operations to achieve customer satisfaction. The ideal state value stream map reflects a process in a perfect state whereby only value-added operations and activities exist.

Value stream maps, whether the current, future, or ideal states, usually contain several elements.

A *process* is the first element. A process consists of one or more operations to provide a product or service to a customer. Each process has a processing time which is the amount of time that a product or service requested by a customer is being designed and built to meet requirements. A process often has a process owner who is the person, usually at a high level in an organization, responsible for the execution and output of a process. One or more processes can make up a value stream.

An *operation* is another key element. One or more operators are embedded in a process. It consists of one or more activities that stakeholders perform to execute a process. The performance of an operation with other ones can affect the performance of a process, negatively or positively, and indeed, the entire flow of a value stream. Flow, more specifically continuous flow, is the ongoing uninterrupted execution of an element, for example, an activity or machine, within an operation and thus a process. Ideally, under Lean, the goal is to have no waste that interferes with the delivery of a product or service to the customer.

Another key element of a value stream map is the *customer*, perhaps the most important one. A customer is the person or organization that receives the output of a process or a value stream. Under Lean, the customer is king. Anything that does not add value to achieving customer satisfaction is waste. Customer satisfaction is the outcome of a process or value stream that meets requirements.

Another key element of a value stream is the supplier, also known as a vendor or contractor. These are people or organizations that are part of the value stream, providing a component or service contributing to the final delivery of a product or service to the customer. In some value streams, many suppliers can participate with the person or organization having overall responsibility for executing a process or value stream. The person or organization having overall responsibility functions as an integrator of the suppliers' contributions. As one would expect, the failure of a supplier can afffect the continuous flow of a value stream and negatively affect customer satisfaction.

These maps provide a wealth of data and information from which to define the current value stream and then to identify opportunities for improvement. They consist of symbols and numbers to define the current, future, and ideal states of a value stream. These symbols are often in the form of what people have used in information technology and process improvement projects in the past as well as road maps to explain business processes. These systems are often used to reflect operations, transportation or movement, decisions, inspections, delays, storage, direction of flow, transmission, suppliers, customers, and recording comments. One unique symbol is the kaizen burst, something of a miniature explosion, indicating and capturing an improvement idea that can help reduce flow time, decrease instability, and improve quality in a process, operation, procedure, or activity. The value stream map also captures related data and information concerning the value stream, under review for one or more procedures, operations, or activities. Data and information may include, but not be limited to, cycle, lead, and queue times; data and information requirements; labor and nonlabor requirements for availability or nonavailability; setup or changeover times; transportation distance and travel time; and quality requirements and defects.

Value stream maps, as described above, are just one way to analyze process flows. The standard process flowchart, SIPOC (suppler, input, process, output, and customer) flowcharting, swim lane charting, interrelationship digraphs, data flow diagramming, and spaghetti charts are additional ways to display a value stream. A *SIPOC chart* describes the relationship of five named elements within a value stream. A *spaghetti chart* is a diagram displaying the route that a product proceeds on through the value stream, traveling from one operation to another. A *data flow diagram* displays the flow of data among different categories of processes and different entities. An *interrelationship digraph* shows dependencies among different processes and entities using input and output arrows to ascertain the greatest impacts on a process from a cause and effect perspective. A *swim lane chart* is a flow chart showing the sequence of events of processes, decisions, and the like as they pertain to the different responsibilities of people or organizations.

Selecting the appropriate documenting approvals depends on familiarity with the technique, complexity of the process, and scale of application. A number of quality control tools can be used with any of the techniques chosen to display the current, To-Be, and ideal states. These basic quality control tools include cause and effect diagrams, check sheets, Pareto charts, histograms, statistical process control charts, scatter plots, affinity diagrams, and matrices, all of which are discussed in further detail along with others. For purposes of this book, value stream mapping is the preferred choice of describing the current, To-Be, and ideal states.

With the necessary data, information, and symbols, the team can review the current value stream to determine where waste occurs. Waste is defined as operations or activities that generate output that provides little or no value to the customer; it is also described as non-value-added. There are often seven forms of waste that might exist in a value stream: overproduction, overprocessing, excess inventory, waiting, rework or corrections, unnecessary transportation, and needless movement. Safety is the eighth form of waste that has recently been added to the list by many Lean practitioners. When identified in the current value stream map, these provide opportunities to identify where to make improvements and build both the future and ideal value stream maps.

Waste in a process can take one of three forms: muda, mura, and muri which are Japanese terms (refer to Figure 4.6). *Muda* is any activity or item in a value stream that does not add value, meaning the customer ascribes no importance to an aspect of a product or service in satisfying its requirements. Muda consists of operations, activities, and so on for which the customer is not willing to pay.

Not all muda is bad, of course, just because it does not add direct value. Known as Type 1 and Type 2, the former consists of those operations and

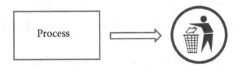

Waste
- Muda (Type 1)
- Mura
- Muri

FIGURE 4.6
Three categories of waste.

activities that are non-value-added but still are important enough to the value stream, such as compliance with regulations. The latter are what really need elimination right from the start. Naturally, Type 2 muda goes first, followed by Type 1.

Mura is the second form of waste. This waste is reflected in the unevenness, or variation, in flow. A perfect example is an unleveled histogram showing an erratic high usage period of resources followed by a low usage period. Mura results in wasteful changeover and setup times or high inventory levels, to name two consequences. Mura should be kept to a minimum, just as with muda.

Muri is the third form of waste. This type of waste places extreme stress on part or all of a system, such as on people and equipment. The results are often burnout and breakdowns, whether an animate or inanimate resource. A perfect example of muri is safety problems resulting from people using equipment after working excessive levels of overtime.

Takt time is the key for dealing with muri and with the other two types of waste for that matter. The goal with takt time is to align production pace with customer demand. Takt time is calculated by dividing production time by the rate of customer demand. This alignment helps to reduce waste by providing a more predictable leveled application of resources.

Lean seeks to reduce and eventually eliminate muda, mura, and muri. Reducing and eliminating all three can result in a more efficient and effective flow based upon pull by the customer rather than push by the producer.

Some common areas to look for opportunities to remove waste and improve quality include records, procedures, training, media, specifications, designs, quality methods, and relationships with suppliers and the customer. The key is to not overlook any opportunity to remove waste. If an opportunity for removing waste arises at any time, a common practice is to record it on the map using a symbol known as a kaizen burst to capture the improvement idea.

Reviewing the current value stream map reveals many areas containing waste. They are often caused by several generic factors affecting the continuous flow of a process.

A constraint is one generic factor. It is any restriction that limits a potentially high performance level of a process or operation. An example might be a policy or procedure that restricts procurement activities of key stakeholders. Constraints can be tangible, such as purchases above a certain level require capital approval from executive leadership or intangible, such as culturally accepted ways to conduct business.

Closely allied with a constraint is an impediment. An *impediment* is a business or technical issue, problem, or other concern that negatively affects and restricts the continuous flow of a process. An example of an impediment might be an uncooperative labor force that continually threatens to, or actually does, sabotage outsourcing agreements. Another example of an impediment is senior management requiring approvals for even the smallest level of expenditures due to a lack of trust in its mid- to lower-level management.

Another generic factor that may have an impact on the continuous flow of a process is the lead time. In the context of Lean, lead time is the cumulative time a customer must wait to receive the final product after submitting an order or request. Lead time can seriously affect the delivery of a product or service especially in an environment where the customer wants it faster, better, and cheaper. Too long a lead time, more than what competitors offer, is a surefire way to lose business. Lead time is not just for the delivery of a product or service. For example, a long lead time to receive resources from suppliers to produce interim deliverables can also affect the overall delivery of a product or service. The shorter the lead times for interim deliverables that make up the final product or service also results in an overall faster delivery to the customer, thereby sustaining or advancing competitive advantage.

Changeover or setup times are another generic factor that may affect the continuous flow of a process. *Changeover* is the transfer from a current operation to another one. Jumping from one operation to another affects the continuous flow in several ways. People take time to get up to speed on the new operation as well as ceasing work on the current operation. Sometimes, people may have to switch back and forth from one operation or activity to another which takes additional time and effort to get back up to speed once again. Too many changeovers can result in delays and mistakes. By reducing the number and length of changeovers the less chance of a significant interruption of the continuous flow of a process.

Another generic factor that can interrupt the continuous flow of a process is the lack of standard work operations or activities. Standard work requires following a common approach, toolset, and techniques. Through standard work, people communicate more effectively and efficiently with each other, know what is expected of them, can clearly understand the impact of an impediment or constraint on a process flow, and more easily identify opportunities for eliminating any of the different forms of waste.

4.3 DEFINE REQUIREMENTS

As mentioned many times already, Lean is a customer-focused approach that concentrates on providing value by eliminating waste and increasing quality. It is important, therefore, to know the customer quite well in order to eliminate waste and increase quality. A major way to do that is to understand the customer's requirements.

Requirements are the criteria that the customer deems of value that the producer or service-provider must satisfy. Addressing the criteria can result in customer satisfaction, which is the outcome of a process providing a product or service that meets customer requirements. These requirements are captured in various forms, which are commonly described in a requirements document or specification or model, also known as a prototype. Models, of course, do not need to have a look and feel per se. A model can be diagrams reflecting processes, procedures, and components of a system, among others, as a way to improve understanding and developing ideas. In the end, the To-Be and ideal state value stream maps are models of the future; the current value stream is a model of what presently exists.

The inability to capture requirements adequately can result in a host of problems and challenges for any Lean endeavor. These problems and challenges include poor communications, lack of teaming, incomplete deliverables or services being delivered, general frustration, conflict among significant stakeholders, constant rework, blown schedules and costs, scope creep, and much more. In many situations, the customer, not just the project team, has no idea what is needed and wanted and, yet, someone has to take the initiative to determine the requirements exactly.

Tools

- Benchmarking
- Cause-and-Effect diagrams
- Control charts
- Frequency plots
- Pareto chart
- Scatter plots
- Tree diagrams
- Etc.

Data ⟹

⟹ Information

FIGURE 4.7
Data collection and analysis.

An important concept of requirements satisfaction is the voice of the customer, or VOC (shown in Figure 4.7). The VOC is collecting the explicit and implicit needs, wants, desires, and expectations of the customer and then translating that information into a requirements specification. According to Lean, the customer is the focus; VOC plants the customer right in the center. It then becomes easier to identify criticality to quality characteristics, that is, activities or deliverables that the customer deems important to achieve the necessary level of satisfaction. There is a decision-making approach known as quality function deployment (QFD) that involves a multidisciplinary team focusing on customer needs and expectations early on in a value stream and provides measurable consistent performance. The use of burnup and burndown charts plays a significant role in counting up or down, respectively, requirements that result in customer satisfaction. A *burndown chart* is the completion rate of deliverables, for example, deliverables over a period of time; a *burnup chart* is the accumulation of deliverables completed, for example, deliverables over a given time period. A *deliverable* is a completed artifact that results in the delivery of the final product or service to a customer. Using burnup or -down charts as they relate to deliverables enables a measureable count to determine progress toward meeting the customer.

For many years, capturing requirements and distinguishing between what is and is not important has been a real challenge. Albeit it remains so today, requirements challenges exist to a lesser degree. Technology has enabled building a prototype, which is a model of the final deliverable or service that will provide customer satisfaction. From a Lean perspective, value stream maps serve as models to define current and future states. Anything that is non-value-added is waste and can result in poor quality. The transition from one model to another is largely based upon pull rather than push. *Pull* means moving information, resources, and so on from the end of the value stream to its beginning based upon receiving a signal to deliver a product or service. *Push* means moving information, resources, and the like from the beginning of the value stream to its end. The move from the current state to the To-Be and ideal states is one of moving from push to pull and reducing and eliminating waste interfering with the transition.

When developing value stream maps or any other types of documentation describing the current, To-Be, and ideal states, keep the following thoughts in mind. One, always have the right stakeholders participate in developing and reviewing documents: they should be people who have a good knowledge of the value stream and can offer useful insights for improvement. Two, avoid the tendency toward myopia: make sure that the stakeholders represent a good cross-section of all the disciplines participating in the value stream. Three, avoid cluttering the maps: consider showing information, not irrelevant data. If the flows get too complex, then stakeholders begin to tune out. Four, keep the flows on maps current. If the content gets dated for whatever reason, the maps start to lose their value and fail to serve as baselines for identifying areas of improvement. Five, strive for completeness in content. Models, by their very nature, are incomplete, and about the only way to compensate for that is to have the right stakeholders review each map and give their approval or disapproval. Six, and finally, frequently reference the maps. By doing so, it will help to ensure that the content is current but also that the Lean project stays focused on the end result. Remember, maps are more than a repository of data and information to reference throughout a Lean project. They also serve as a road map to guide the team from concept to reality by delivering a product or service to satisfy the customer by meeting requirements.

Once captured in a document, often called a specification, requirements are set as a baseline, which, in this context, serves as an agreement among two or more stakeholders. The baseline becomes the target. From a Lean perspective, all three value stream maps are set as baselines, meaning any changes will need to undergo evaluation as to impact, such as financial, schedule, and scope.

4.4 COLLECT DATA AND INFORMATION

A map shows the flow of data and information, and other resources, from the beginning of the value stream to the end. The flow itself can prove invaluable; however, additional data and information are usually needed to come up with recommendations for improvement after reviewing the current value stream map.

It is important to note, before proceeding, that a difference exists between data and information. *Data* are facts that have no meaning. *Information* is meaningful, that is, data analyzed and converted into content of value to a recipient. Collecting data for data's sake is wasteful; collecting data to come up with information to produce or provide something of value is meaningful. Through value stream analysis, the goal is to collect useful data that will result in meaningful information which, in turn, leads toward determining opportunities for improvement. The current value stream is the vehicle to collect data and provide information on an existing process.

When collecting data and analyzing a value stream, consider following a few simple, often overlooked, guidelines. Failure to follow these guidelines can translate into erroneous information that can result in poorly formulated recommendations or overlooked meaningful improvements. These threats include introducing bias into the selection of data, treating unproven assumptions as facts during information interpretation, collecting an insufficient sample size from a given population, treating correlations as cause-and-effect relationships, the approach used to collect data or the collector's characteristics influences results, not clearly articulating definitions prior to data collection, and treating a dependent variable as an independent one and vice versa.

Whatever the challenge with collecting data and drawing conclusions, take some important preventive steps. One, define all terms, also called operationalizing. Examples include terms such as customer satisfaction, where interpretation can vary wildly. Two, "scrub" data before conversion into information, such as ensuring no duplicates exist and that each datum reflects the same level of consistent quality, such as within a reasonable time period. Three, list and verify assumptions or at least be conscious of them in order to avoid introducing bias during collection. Four, be mindful of drawing false conclusions, such as saying a causal relationship exists among data when, in reality, it is correlative. Five, apply data stratification, that is, divide data into smaller populations to facilitate analysis and reporting while being mindful, of course, that the decision of where to stratify may influence results. The key is to strive for objectivity and minimize subjectivity when collecting data and converting the sample into information.

Striving for objectivity makes it easier to ascertain the root cause for why something occurs, whether a defect or an event. A root cause is defined as a "real" factor that contributes to an outcome; by identifying the root cause it can then be influenced or manipulated to achieve a desired result.

Some data are necessary to conduct analyses of the current value stream, make improvements, and follow up with some measurements to verify and validate effectiveness.

Throughput time is one datum. It is the combination of processing and queue time for a product or service being delivered to a customer. These data provide a reliable measure of improvement in terms of time of delivery to the customer. By reducing throughput time more timely delivery is possible, assuming, of course, no degradation of quality occurs.

Defect rate is also an important datum. Defect rate is the number of occurrences within a given time period. The goal is to reduce the rate of defects by implementing recommendations to ensure that quality remains the same or improves.

Inventory levels are important, too. Under Lean, inventory levels add to overhead. The goal is to reduce overhead. It is important, therefore, to have accurate data on inventory and to ascertain, after the improvements have been made, whether inventory levels have decreased.

Unit costs are important as well. Unit costs can include labor or non-labor. Ideally, unit costs should decrease as the overhead declines, allowing pricing to the customer to remain, or become even more, competitive. Improvements often result in more competitive pricing or greater returns to investors.

The above data and others can help identify opportunities for improvement by helping to pinpoint problems in the seven areas of waste mentioned earlier: transportation, waiting, overproduction, defects, inventory, motion, and excess processing. As mentioned earlier, an eighth form of waste has now been identified: safety.

With the data collected, several tools are available to display the results. Some of the more common tools are described below (refer to Figure 4.8).

- *Benchmarking* is the technique of comparing a company's performance in a process with companies considered "best-in-class" and then improving process performance accordingly.
- *Cause-and-effect diagrams* are used to display the relationships, for example, causal or correlative, among two or more variables. A

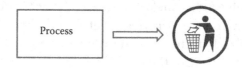

Wastes
- Poorly motivated workforce
- Inadequate or no communications
- Lack of coordination
- Changeover times
- Large backlogs
- Excess inventory
- Defects
- Excessive lead times
- Long queue times
- Safety problems

FIGURE 4.8
Non-value-added waste examples.

common cause-and-effect diagram is the fishbone diagram identifying causes grouped in several categories and displaying how they cause or contribute to a problem, issue, and so on.

- *Control charts* visually display information showing patterns of behavior over a period of time. A common control chart is statistical process control (SPC), reflecting dispersion around the mean, acceptable, and unacceptable specification limits.
- A *frequency plot* is used to display how often an event occurs. A check sheet is an example of a frequency plot.
- A *Pareto chart* is a graphical display showing the frequency of occurrence of an event or categories of events vis-à-vis other events or categories. The Pareto chart helps to determine the cause of a problem or issue by displaying the data in the form of a histogram.
- *Scatter plots*, also known as scatter-grams, are tools showing the relationship, casual or correlative, between two factors. The idea behind the display of data points is to ascertain the degree of relationship by looking at the tightness of the dispersion.
- *Tree diagrams* are graphical tools to display the relationships among multiple variables, usually from a top-down perspective. An example of a tree diagram is a network diagram showing the relationship among different variables based upon probability or likelihood and impact.

4.5 PERFORM ANALYSIS

Using the data collected, the Lean project team can then start conducting its analysis. This principally requires reviewing the current value stream map and associated data to determine any opportunities to eliminate waste.

Waste, to reiterate, consists of operations or activities that generate output but provide little or no value to the customer. Another term for waste is non-value-added and the Japanese term is muda. The review should result in identifying impediments and constraints that contribute to waste and cause the process or processes in the value stream map to "choke," thereby resulting in waste.

The goal is to eliminate all forms of waste which is frequently categorized in these eight areas: transportation, waiting, overproduction, defects, inventory, motion, excess processing, and, recently added, safety. Although all eight categories are presented as if independent of each other, yet they are more like Venn diagrams, overlapping. For example, overproduction and defects can lead to excess inventories, which, in turn, lead to waiting. Seeing these interrelationships among some of the categories is possible with a value stream map by enabling assessment of the subsequent impact on internal operations and activities and, ultimately, the customer. Reviewing the value stream map enables analysis to focus on identifying and fixing the root cause and not simply address the symptoms.

While conducting the analysis when reviewing the value stream, it is important always to ask the following questions: What is the goal of this process, operation, or activity? Who performs this process, operation, or activity? When does this process, operation, or activity start and stop and where is its sequence relative to the others in the value stream map? Where does this process, operation, or activity occur? How is this process, operation, or activity conducted, for example, manually and automated? Perhaps, most important, the following should be asked: Why? This question may be the hardest of all to ask because it leads to the heart of the analysis by challenging the status quo and could, quite frankly, lead toward eliminating what is considered a sacrosanct process, operation, or activity. A common way to ask that question is to apply the technique of asking why five times (and sometimes even more depending on the complexity). Why? Why? Why? Why? Why? Anyone with very young children knows what that is like because they always ask that question. The same principle applies here. The notion is that by asking why so many times a person or team can eventually identify the root cause of a problem.

In some cases, it may be worthwhile to develop additional charts that can supplement or complement a value stream map. A spaghetti chart can help reveal the route that a product or deliverable takes through a value stream. If it shows a circuitous pattern then that may provide an opportunity for improvement. Documenting a milk run where a transport vehicle makes multiple pickups at several locations, for example, can be captured in a spaghetti chart.

Another useful diagram is one that shows the layout of a work cell. A work cell is a multidisciplinary cross-functional arrangement of people, machines, and other resources to produce a product or service. The arrangement of resources can reveal opportunities for improvement.

The important point is that the value stream map is a tool to conduct analysis but it does not preclude the use of other techniques to conduct greater analyses, especially as one drills down into a specific process, operation, or activity. The value stream serves as a road map for improvement within and among processes, operations, or activities.

Armed with data and a map, an analysis can be conducted to determine the true cause of waste (refer to Figure 4.9). This requires reviewing the flow of a value stream to determine at what point waste occurs. In Lean jargon, this analysis is sometimes referred to as turnback analysis. A team goes through the map doing a forward and backward pass looking at the data and identifying any areas that could cause waste. It requires looking at the linkage among processes, operations, or activities to determine the cause of impact on each one and then ascertaining which ones may possibly be the cause. After identifying the opportunities for waste, the time arises to drill down to determine the cause. This approach requires using several tools to perform analysis, such as the ones discussed earlier, for example, Pareto charts.

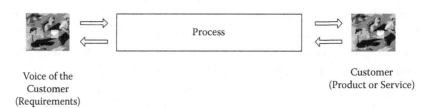

Voice of the
Customer
(Requirements)

Customer
(Product or Service)

FIGURE 4.9
Voice of the customer.

Here are some problems to look for when conducting an analysis. Many of these problems were discussed earlier but should be mentioned once again only because they are often the most salient and prevalent ones popping up in a value stream. Be advised, once again, these are not mutually exclusive and the existence of one type of waste can be the result of another existing one.

Excessive inventory. These are parts, products, data, and other items that remain incomplete or unneeded at least for the moment. However, they can also include complete items that are piled up to deal with such problems as an inability to ascertain customer demand or to handle returns for whatever reason, for example, defects. Needless inventory results in increased overhead that adds costs passed on to the customer and ultimately affects competitive pricing. Excessive inventory may be the result of overproduction or poor transportation.

Defects. A defect, from a Lean perspective, is the output from a process, operation, or activity that potentially dashes a customer's expectations, resulting in customer dissatisfaction. Defects can occur in a product or service. The goal, of course, is to reduce defects; too many of them not only result in customer dissatisfaction but also require substantial overhead by requiring a just-in-case inventory, litigation and warranty costs, poor reputability, and loss of market share. Defects also create a loss of confidence by everyone in the value stream, reflecting some serious underlying problems among key stakeholders participating in the process, operation, or activity in question.

Excessive lead time. In an international economy where resources may be coming from all over the world and assembled into a final product being delivered to a customer or providing a service, lead times are inevitable. The problem is that sometimes, if excessive, lead times can delay delivery to a customer. If a competitor can deliver sooner and provide an equal if not better product or service, all things being equal, the customer will prefer having output sooner rather than later. Lead times often result from erratic transportation and motion by key stakeholders in the value stream.

Long queue time. This one is the amount of time a resource, part, product, or service waits to proceed forward in a value stream. The longer the queue time is, usually, the slower the delivery of the product or service to the customer. Excessive queue time often results in many forms of waste. There is idle time as resources pile up creating excessive inventories, often described as batch-and-queue time, whereby parts, products, and the like are accumulated in large lots that are subsequently placed in a queue for use in a process, operation, or activity in the future. There is the chance resources decay, if perishable, requiring disposal, thereby adding to overhead. There is the challenge of overproduction, adding even more to overhead, with the excess inventory exceeding customer needs. Queue time may be coupled with lead time: if one is out of sync with the other then it can lead to excessive, or too little, inventory. Either way, the result is costly. The goal is to time production according to takt time, whereby production is in time with customer demand.

Large backlogs. This one is another area to investigate. A backlog is an accumulation of a workload with content that remains open, has not been prioritized, and is scheduled for fixing. These are often issues, problems, or improvements that need to be addressed but nothing has happened. Backlogs result in poor performance in a value stream because they remain unresolved. If left unattended, they can affect the quality of output and result in additional waste, such as rework and large inventories to provide a "quick fix" to a long-standing problem. Often, backlogs are the result of key stakeholders more interested in putting out fires, so to speak, than in addressing root causes. Failure to address backlogs, if they become really serious, can affect relations with the customer once they realize that the price paid for the product or service is padded to account for the waste resulting from not addressing backlog issues.

Changeover times. This is the time to transfer from one current process, operation, or activity to a new different one. As mentioned earlier, the goal is to reduce that time because it provides greater flexibility for responding to different situations. The more time for the transfer to occur, the greater the loss of productivity and an extension of the flow time for a value stream. This situation becomes a significant problem in work cells whereby people may have to shift to different tools and equipment. Stopping to proceed from one process, operation, or activity often requires either learning something new or getting up to speed, let alone increasing the need for better coordination and communication among stakeholders.

There are, of course, less tangible problems that may surface when reviewing a value stream. These are harder to identify but with a little more effort can be discernible by looking at the consequences of each one.

Lack of coordination. Synchronization is very important in a value stream; all stakeholders must work together to ensure efficient and effective performance. Any semblance of a lack of coordination results in waste. One process, operation, or activity that fails to work in concert with another to deliver a product or service to a customer typifies a lack of coordination. Engineering and manufacturing, for example, sometimes fail to work hand in hand to develop a part or component for technical equipment that will be delivered to the customer. Lack of coordination is often reflected in defects and failing to meet customer specifications. It can also result in excessive inventories to compensate for a lack of coordination. Finally, it can cause considerable rework.

Inadequate or no communication. Arguably, all of the above problems are the result of inadequate or no communication. During a large, complex value stream, this problem can manifest through rework, a lack of coordination, and defective workmanship because specifications were not clearly communicated or not communicated at all. Excessive inventories could also be the result of compensating for these shortcomings. In a value stream, the upstream processes, operations, and activities frequently communicate poorly with the downstream ones. According to Lean theory, a customer's expectations are the drivers; however, if the information is misinterpreted or lost, pull is not possible. Everyone in the value stream must communicate consistently and persistently by sharing data and information to the maximum extent possible. A large part of those data and information centers on customer expectations and knowing what other stakeholders do in the value stream.

Poorly motivated workforce. Like safety, this one is a new addition to the seven forms of waste, now taking the total to nine. Safety is the eighth and is discussed next. A poorly motivated workforce does, indeed, lead to waste. People will likely not perform efficiently and effectively, resulting in unwanted inventories, defects resulting in rework, poor coordination, inadequate or no communication, and excessive waiting. How does one determine if the cause is a poorly motivated workforce? Look for clues, including negative conflict, people reluctant to share essential information, gridlock in the value stream, and turnover, just to mention a few. A poorly motivated workforce may be due to many tangible reasons, such as poor pay, as well as intangible ones, such as a lack of growth. Regardless of the reason, look for the indicators just described because a poorly motivated workforce can result in considerable waste in a value stream and may not always be discernible.

Safety problems. This problem has recently been added, too. Safety is a major concern because it deals with the health and welfare of stakeholders involved in a value stream. People are, indeed, the greatest resource in an organization because they apply the skills, knowledge, and experience to deliver a product or service to a customer. If stakeholders doing the work in a value stream are hurt, they cannot produce, leading to many other problems that result in waste: excessive queue and lead times, rework, defects, inadequate and poor communication, and lack of coordination. Safety problems are relatively easier to detect by tracking loss of work days due to injuries on the job, employees filing lawsuits due to working conditions, and the number of sick days taken by employees. It is important to note that these statistics may be due to other causes but also serve as indicators that people may not feel physically and, just as important, psychologically safe at work.

4.6 APPLY TOOLS AND TECHNIQUES FOR SOLUTIONS

A Lean project team began developing potential solutions to address the different forms of waste (refer to Figure 4.10). It understood the context, developed the value stream, identified requirements, collected data and converted them to information, and performed analysis to determine the problems or issues to address leading to both future and ideal states in a value stream. What follows is a high-level description of tools and techniques to address one or more of the different forms of waste.

✓ Visual signals
✓ Leveling
✓ Defect prevention
✓ Faster changeover
✓ Improved maintenance
✓ Enhanced communications
✓ Physical layout
✓ Better coordination
✓ Greater standardized work
✓ Contingency preparations
✓ Safety enhancement
✓ Increase stakeholder motivation

FIGURE 4.10
Ways to cut waste.

Visual signals provide an effective means to improve performance. They not only improve communication but also coordination and adapting to situations. Kanban is a common signal system that manages or regulates the flow of resources through the value stream by notifying upstream processes, operations, and activities. Kanban is predicated on using visual indicators for stakeholders to indicate performance status. An *andon* is one such visual status signal system that indicates the status of a process and when a problem arises through its execution. This information is often coupled with a control chart that visually displays information showing patterns of behavior over a period of time. Another effective signaling tool is the dashboard that visually displays reports on progress, trends, and potential risks. In the end, the goal is to display information with self-explanatory content about status; this tool is often referred to by Lean practitioners as an information radiator. Visual signals are useful for addressing all forms of waste but are especially of value dealing with waiting, overproduction, inventory, excess processing, and defects.

Leveling, more specifically level setting, provides another effective way to improve performance. The idea is to have production occur at a steady pace rather than according to wide variations, referred to as mura in Japanese, that can lead to what is known as work in progress inventory and other wasteful practices. Leveling requires profiling a process, in addition to the product, to the customer to reduce surges in demand while at the same time satisfy its requirements. The goal is to reduce the spread of the peaks and valleys that accompany demand in traditional production environments. By communicating and coordinating with the customer, production can meet demand in a steady predictable manner according to takt time, which is having production pace aligned with customer demand. The Japanese term for leveling is *heijunka*, which seeks to reduce variation in production to attain a smooth process flow. A tool, called a heijunka box, is used to control production via kanban at fixed time intervals. With leveling, it becomes easier to adopt manufacturing approaches that seek timely delivery of products and services and the components that make them. One such approach is just-in-time (JIT) delivery, whereby the right amount of resources is delivered at the right time at the right place, thereby reducing work in process and allowing for continuous flow. Leveling helps to address several forms of waste to include inventory, waiting, and overproduction.

Defect prevention is delivering as much as possible an error-free product or service and, if one arises, then keeping it out of the hands of the customer.

Poka-yoke is Japanese for a procedure or device applied to prevent an error or defect from moving forward in the value stream and ending up delivered to the customer. The way to do that, of course, is to build quality into the process, operation, or activity so that inspections downstream are reduced and that customer returns are as minimal as possible. The people working on a process, operation, or activity take ownership of the results of their work; that means being responsible for the quality of their output. Quality, in the end, is meeting the specifications of the customer. All the principles of the quality movement apply to Lean; some of these principles include reducing variation, not giving the customer more than what it requested, satisfying real needs, emphasizing prevention over inspection, and pursuing continuous improvement. One way to do that is to apply autonomation, that is, having a system, using an intelligent agent, which enables detecting a production problem; causes the process, operation, or activity to cease; and alerts the need for assistance to achieve resolution. An andon is another tool, discussed earlier, to indicate the status of a process and when a problem arises during its execution. Defect prevention helps to address several forms of waste, including inventory, defects, and extra processing.

Faster changeover is about speed. Also known as single minute exchange of dies (SMED), the idea is to expedite the transition from one set of activities to another. The goals are to reduce that time by a significant percent as well as decrease the number of steps. That way more can be processed through the value stream quickly and in larger quantities. Too many steps causes delays and confusion and are augmented each time a changeover occurs. Ideally, a one-touch setup is the end state, whereby any changeover requires a short time to occur. By improving changeovers, several forms of waste are reduced or eliminated, including waiting, inventory, and motion which translate into faster, more continuous value stream performance and reduced costs.

Improved maintenance at first seems to focus on maintaining the status quo. However, nothing could be further from the truth. Through what is known as total productive maintenance, or TPM, considerable energy is spent by the employees to ensure that equipment is kept in working order. Employees must take personal responsibility for monitoring and caring for their equipment; management provides the necessary support as well as provides relevant data and information about the equipment. Three variables are considered when applying TPM to equipment: availability, that is, the amount of uptime; performance, whether it is operating at an acceptable level of capacity; and quality, the degree of producing defect-free output. Other variables might include failure, or downtime rates, and mean time between failures. Not all equipment need be subject to TPM; however, it is best to apply TPM on critical processes, operations, and activities in the value stream, especially if a failure to perform can create choke points, or bottlenecks. Through improved maintenance, several forms of waste are reduced or affected, to include inventory, waiting, and safety.

Enhanced communications rarely, if ever, fails to improve performance. As mentioned earlier, visual signals play an instrumental role in enhancing communication throughout a value stream by applying techniques such as kanban and andon. A dashboard, or information radiator, is a visual display providing reports on progress, trends, and other concerns (e.g., potential risks) that can serve as an effective communication tool. A dashboard can be electronic or hardcopy, preferably the former because Lean stresses the importance of using automation. The content should be self-explanatory and provide only the essential elements of information. Another effective communication tool is what is called A3. An *A3* is simply a summary document, no more than one page, which contains critical information about a process or project. It might describe a problem or issue, the actions to take or that have been taken, the status to date, and its goals and objectives. It may also include any other useful information. Still another effective tool, and one that often is not popular but sure can get people to communicate and coordinate fairly quickly, is the daily stand-up meeting. This meeting should take no more than 20 minutes and is simply a means to share information regarding their responsibilities. The purpose is to communicate, not solve problems. Other tools that have been discussed earlier that can enhance communication in a value stream include performing gemba which involves visitation at the location where work is actually being performed to enhance understanding and learn when to add value to the customer; modeling, such as building a prototype prior to full production to increase communication about requirements and expectations; applying the voice of the customer, collecting the explicit and implicit needs, wants, and desires and expectations, and translating that information into requirements and specifications; applying quality function deployment, assembling a multidisciplinary team to focus on customer needs and expectations; and doing validation, checking with the customer to ascertain whether a product or service satisfies customer requirements and expectations. Remember: enhanced communication reduces or eliminates all forms of waste, including safety and an unmotivated workforce.

Improved physical layout is a significant contributor to reducing waste. Typically, work areas are arranged by what is known as batch-and-queue, that is, the accumulation of parts, products, and so on in large lots that will subsequently be placed in queue for use in a process, operation, or activity in the future. Large inventories are created as a result of batch processing as well as creating a substantial work-in-process, adding to space for storage and overhead costs. Continuous flow is not often possible, at least on a regular basis, in a batch-and-queue arrangement. By reconfiguring machinery, equipment, seating, and the like in a counterclockwise configuration, continuous flow becomes more feasible. Creating such a work cell requires a multidisciplinary cross-functional arrangement of people, machines, and other resources to produce a product or deliver a service. It also requires worker training to operate different types of equipment via cross-training, a practice commonly referred to as multimachine working. To ensure continuous flow, visual control systems, such as a kanban, are used to move output from one workstation to the next. The idea is to keep the flow moving continuously at a consistent steady pace within each cell and throughout the overall process or operation rather than having it proceed sporadically with incessant starts and stops, resulting in work-in-process inventory. This requires, of course, considerable planning with the customer to incorporate lead times to meet demand on a pull, rather than push, basis. Improving the physical layout helps to reduce several forms of waste, including transportation, waiting, inventory, overproduction, and motion.

Better coordination is achievable by applying several tools and techniques. Coordination works hand in hand with communication. A failure in coordination is more often than not a failure in communication; a failure in communication is more often than not a failure in coordination. Perhaps the easiest way to ascertain if coordination is a problem in a value stream is to produce a spaghetti chart, a diagram displaying the route by which a product proceeds through a value stream, often revealing its circuitous travel from one operation to another. Or, a spaghetti chart might be developed for a milk run, which is using a transport medium, such as a van or truck, involving multiple pickups or dropoffs or both at several locations. Benchmarking might be used, a technique to compare a company's performance in a process of a similar vein with companies considered "best-in-class" to identify opportunities to improve performance.

These companies may employ a best practice that is superior to the methods or practices being employed currently and can be applied where relevant within the value stream. Still another technique is to apply tollgates, specifically identified meetings with stakeholders at certain stages within a process, operation, or activity or phases of a project to determine if requirements and expectations are being met and, if so, continue on or, if not, pursue a change in direction. Better coordination addresses just about all forms of waste but, more specifically, transportation, waiting, inventory, motion, and excess processing.

Greater standardized work is a critical technique to reduce waste. Unfortunately, standardization often generates fear among some people when, in fact, it should do just the opposite. People misconstrue it as a threat to creativity and independence and visions of robotic performance on the job cloud everybody's minds. This is a common misconception. In fact, standardization actually liberates people in a value stream. Without standardization in a complex value stream, stakeholders are constantly spending non-value-added time trying to unravel and translate different ways of doing business for the same desired outcome. They find themselves constantly having to do rework to accommodate other stakeholders because the work performed upstream is not in sync with the requirements downstream. Standardization can improve the value stream at all levels, from processes to activities. The best tool to achieve greater standardization is to apply 5S. *Five S* consists of these elements: sort, straighten, scrub, systematize, and standardize. *Sort* is determining what to keep or discard; *straighten*, placing all important equipment, supplies, information, and so on in an assigned location that does not disrupt the workflow; *scrub*, cleaning nonlabor resources and inspecting them for problems; *systematize*, following a regular ongoing schedule for applying 5S; and *standardize*, instilling 5S into the workforce by applying it through all processes, operations, and activities. Standardization helps to reduce or eliminate all seven forms of waste.

Contingency preparation is still another way to reduce waste. Some events or scenarios can arise for just about any process, operation, or activity in the value stream. The key is to try to identify all the scenarios as much as possible and have a contingency plan in place to deal with each one. The basic notion is to prepare in advance so that the disruption to the value stream is minimal. One effective tool that has been around is the failure mode and effect analysis, or FMEA. This technique can be used to identify potential product and process risks or problems that can occur at discrete points in the value stream. These failure modes, as they are called, are really risks and potential problems that can be dealt with by taking preventive action or responding effectively they should arise. For each scenario, be it a risk or problem, the potential effects are determined and recorded. They assess the consequence, probability or likelihood, and ease of detection to determine a priority to the scenario. An appropriate response is made to eliminate or to reduce the impact of an applicable failure mode. An action plan is then developed to identify and implement appropriate responses for each failure mode. Naturally, not all risks or problems can be anticipated. Most of the time, however, techniques such as FMEA can help to capture and respond to the ones that have a good chance of occurring; that way the value stream can flow as continuously as possible. Contingency preparation can help reduce or eliminate waste for transportation, waiting, defects, inventory, and safety.

Safety enhancement is often overlooked as a way to reduce or eliminate waste. Yet, this failure to recognize its importance can lead to substantial waste in a value stream. Not only can overlooking safety lead to litigation because of noncompliance and loss of work days due to accidents, injuries, and medical restrictions, it also can have an impact in less tangible ways, specifically psychological. The fear of injury can inhibit people from performing at full capacity. As a result, people become overly cautious. It's not just the people doing the work either; other stakeholders may decide to have people working with them be extra cautious simply to avoid responsibility if something does happen under their watch. Not only do people become more cautious but they may also be reluctant to report any safety concerns that could arise simply because of the ramifications associated with their occurrence. Whatever the reason, it makes good business sense to ensure safety is a top priority in a value stream. Otherwise, a safety incident can slow or even halt the continuous flow of a value stream which, in turn leads to waste. Five S is one of the tools to ensure greater safety because it reduces or eliminates waste that may contribute to accidents or injuries. FMEA also helps to identify potential safety concerns and to develop responses accordingly. Visual controls can help bring attention to just about any safety problems or issues that arise when an injury occurs. Safety enhancement can help reduce or eliminate these forms of waste: transportation, waiting, and motion.

Increased stakeholder motivation may seem inconsequential but it helps to resolve value stream impediments that are not always apparent until one of them surfaces and has serious effects. Motivation covers many areas for all kinds of stakeholders. Frederick Herzberg and Abraham Maslow, among many others, have come up with models that describe how people can become, or not become, motivated. Essentially all these models present two major categories of motivators, tangible (e.g., physical) and intangible (e.g., professional growth). The tangible category consists of variables such as money and offices. The intangible variables include recognition and professional achievement. Regardless, if the expectations of tangible and intangible variables are not met, motivation can suffer, even disappear. If such circumstances arise, then stakeholder performance can suffer and affect the value stream. Increasing motivation is difficult to achieve because it often reveals itself when motivation is lacking or in areas where a need for improvement, such as negative conflict, turnover, and safety incidents, exists. There are ways to increase or sustain levels of motivation. Some ways include rewards and recognition at the individual and team levels; encouraging participation and ownership when identifying and implementing improvements; eliminating fear of repercussions for suggesting or implementing changes; ensuring open communications vertically and laterally in the chain of command; and, somewhat related to the last point, building trust among all stakeholders to allow for sharing of thoughts, data, and information. A motivated workforce can eliminate all forms of waste because it is willing to tackle impediments to the continuous flow of the value stream and come up with meaningful ways to satisfy the customer.

4.7 MAKE RECOMMENDATIONS

Using the tools and techniques described above for collecting data and information, performing analysis, and applying tools and techniques for solutions, the time is ripe to formulate recommendations. Making recommendations can take various forms; however, one of the best approaches is to create a situation target proposal, or STP. Before developing the STP, however, two additional value streams require development, the future state value stream map and the ideal state value stream map. The future and ideal state value stream maps, once completed, help to complete the STP.

The STP format is an excellent way to present findings and recommendations to different levels of management to seek approval. This document should be no longer than 10 pages in length, and the higher the presentation goes up the managerial hierarchy, the more brevity matters. There are other advantages, too. It forces a person or a team to articulate the topic sufficiently. It provides a logical sequence to present information that can lead to action. It also provides management, from first levels to the highest levels of the organization, information that is more mentally digestible than if provided with a flood of information. Finally, it serves as an audit trail on why the Lean project exists in the first place.

The first section of the STP is the situation. This section provides mainly background information regarding the reason for a Lean project. This section presents the challenges that exist in the current environment, such as issues, risks, and problems; the symptoms or impacts of these challenges, such as costs, production, and customer service; and the causes of the challenges and symptoms, such as too many approvals, excessive inventories, or too many defects.

The second section of the STP is the target. This section describes the future or ideal states or both. Naturally, an organization will normally progress from one state to the other, albeit that may not necessarily be the case if the leadership seeks radical transformation of a process. This section, therefore, describes the target. This may include a description of the future state and then the ideal one. This section, at a high level, provides background information, discusses the benefits of the applicable state and, if necessary, the impacts on the value stream. It also provides information regarding what will be specifically affected, who will be affected, when the change is necessary, where in the value stream the change will occur, and why the change is needed.

The third section of the STP is the proposal. The second section provides "technical" and business descriptions of what is to change. It presents the game plan to achieve the target. This section also describes the options to achieve the target, the pros and cons of each one (usually displayed in a matrix) from project and business management perspectives, and a recommendation on what to pursue which, incidentally, may include doing nothing. Don't be surprised that a recommendation is rejected or modified by the project sponsor or a steering team. Just be prepared to discuss with them the pros and cons of any revised recommendation. One last page in this section should include a sentence or two to prompt the reviewers to make a decision and what should occur next. A simple title might simply be "Next Steps?" Often, there is a long moment of silence before one or more of the reviewers feels impelled to speak. Remember, the primary purpose of an STP is to call for a decision that results in either moving forward or stopping now.

Here are some secrets of success for preparing and presenting an STP.

Secret number 1 is to keep it clean and simple. Avoid cluttering the pages with detail. Contrary to popular belief, too much detail presented to management does not mean the subject was well thought out. Often it means the opposite, reflecting a lack of clarity about the problem, the vision, and the path to take. The best approach is to limit the number of pages and have the details in what is often referred to as your "hip pocket." If necessary, display the relevant information.

Secret number 2 is to populate the proposal with summary, or rollup, information. This degree of summarization will depend upon the level of management that must grant approval to proceed. A lower level of management will likely want more detail than a higher level. More often than not, give preference to graphics over narrative information. If presenting narrative information, then display the content in bullet lists, such as when giving a slide presentation.

Secret number 3 is to obtain as much feedback as possible from the audience, in draft form, before having the formal meeting. This secret will eliminate any "surprises" from arising during the formal review and allows capturing any questions or objections in advance, thereby allowing the presenter to be totally prepared. It also avoids political surprises to surface if someone of higher rank is in the review along with subordinate managers and executives.

Secret number 4 is to distribute the STP in advance of the approval review session. Two to three days in advance should provide sufficient time for reviewers to prepare themselves and raise any questions or concerns. It also provides the presenter with the opportunity to capture and address any concerns prior to the review session.

4.8 PLAN AND EXECUTE

Assuming that the project sponsor, either an individual or a group acting as a steering committee grants approval to proceed, the next action is to prepare a project plan using the principles, practices, and concepts of PM discussed in the previous chapter.

The plan often requires additional review after the STP to ensure the plan is realistic and has the necessary support to proceed. This subsequent presentation should, at a summary level, explain the reason for the project. Its content should be taken from a draft of the charter, a schedule, such as key milestone dates, significant risks, roles and responsibilities, cost estimates, acceptance criteria, communications plan, and issues and approach for executing the plan. Remember, this information is presented in a summary format. In some cases, a charter may suffice; in other cases, the sponsor or steering committee may require additional information. Be sure to emphasize how change will be managed, as well as verifying that the Lean project focuses on meeting the technical and business requirements through verifications, for example, meeting specific standards to assure compliance with quality standards, and validation, for example, meeting the requirements of the customer.

4.9 LEAN 101

This chapter is not meant to make the reader an expert on Lean. The intent is to give project managers a good understanding of the concepts, tools, and techniques concerning Lean. Project managers need to know the rudiments of Lean to understand what is occurring in regard to the subject. In the subsequent chapters, the focus is on applying PM on two basic life cycles to manage Lean projects: the PDCA and the DMAIC life cycles.

5

Lean and Project Management Processes

Projects have a greater likelihood of success if project management (PM) tools, disciplines, concepts, and principles are applied; they have a lesser chance of success without PM. To leverage the gains from applying PM requires taking a structured rather than haphazard approach. The way to do that is to apply PM processes.

5.1 KEY CONCEPTS

Before discussing the PM processes, however, it is important to set the stage with some concepts that should be considered before any process is implemented.

Define the Lean problem, or issue, as clearly as possible. This definition sets the stage for all subsequent phases and the activities within them. If the definition is vague then the danger of not coming up with one or more solutions that satisfy the customer arises or scope creep becomes such a problem that it results in gold plating, that is, giving the customer more than what is necessary, which, in turn, affects the budget and schedule and may even degrade the quality of the results. Additionally, not defining the issue or problem may result in a project plan that proves unrealistic later in the cycle. Finally, a good definition of the problem or issue will make managing and leading the project much easier.

Avoid being overly ambitious. If a Lean project employs a life cycle for the first time, pick a problem or issue that will not over- or underwhelm people. The problem or issue should be on a scale that presents sufficient challenge and that has a likelihood of success. The best approach is to develop a model or prototype for the potential solution and build upon its progress throughout the life cycle to assess the results. If the model or prototype demonstrates value, then consider expanding the project to develop a full solution to the problem or issue in question. The key is to demonstrate success and to minimize the opportunity for failure. All the key stakeholders gain, by not only learning about Lean and its tools and techniques, but also by having a good opportunity to ascertain if the scale of the issue or problem is appropriate for the project.

Solicit and maintain customer involvement. In the end, a Lean project is about the customer, regardless of whether using the PDCA or DMAIC life cycle. Involving and maintaining customer involvement increases the likelihood of success. After all, the purpose of a Lean project is customer satisfaction by eliminating waste. In many other projects, the customer ceases to become the reason for existence and the project goes off in a different direction. The surest way to keep that focus is to consistently and persistently engage and inform the customer during each phase of a Lean project.

Take a multifunctional approach. Very few Lean projects involve just one discipline, such as engineering or information technology. More often than not, they involve multiple disciplines working together throughout a Lean project. Although each one provides a unique perspective, they seek consensus on both the problem, or issue, and the approach to address it. Stakeholders from each of the various disciplines provide useful insights as well as learn to see problems, or issues, and potential solutions from different perspectives. Any differences are resolved through agreement or consensus by the project manager encouraging each stakeholder to remember what is in the best interests of the customer.

Identify all relevant quality tools and techniques regardless of life cycle. The life cycle of a Lean project is conceptually at a high enough level to allow using a wide range of quality tools and techniques to improve the value stream. Force field analyses, fishbone diagrams, scatter plots, statistical process control, Pareto charts, trend charts, and much more can be applied throughout the life cycle of a Lean project. Even the simplicity of the PDCA cycle does not mean using a limited set of tools and techniques. It does mean, however, being creative and judicious in their application.

Consistently apply the phases of the Lean life cycle. Be sure to follow all phases in the life cycle of a Lean project. Be sure to follow the sequence again and again, if necessary, but do not skip any of the phases. Consistently applying the phases produces steady results because each iteration, if there is more than one, builds upon its predecessor. Skipping over one phase will invariably affect the quality of the output from subsequent phases. If the life cycle repeats itself, it may also weaken the final results of the project.

Involve key stakeholders throughout a Lean project. Getting and keeping stakeholders engaged is absolutely critical throughout a Lean project. Through engagement comes emotional involvement and commitment. When engagement occurs and is sustained, good teaming arises and people are willing to share their knowledge and insights. It also helps in satisfying expectations. The challenge, of course, is sustaining involvement, especially if the life cycle of a project occurs over a lengthy time period.

Determine the degree of PM to apply. Too much PM can hinder the performance of a Lean project. Too little PM will not provide the necessary direction and road map to lead a team to success. The key is to provide the right amount of PM and to do that by working with key stakeholders to determine the extent of project management to employ. Some Lean projects, whether using the PDCA or DMAIC life cycles, may require what is referred to in some circles as *PM lite,* meaning that the degree of PM provides just enough direction and discipline. Others, especially if the scale is much greater, may require a greater degree of PM. The best approach is to obtain consensus from the project sponsor or steering committee, the customer, and the project team.

Recognize the people side. It is easy to get lost in the mechanics of managing a Lean project. The tools and techniques of statistical analysis and value stream mapping, for instance, can prove quite stimulating mentally. However, a Lean project involves people, and the results can affect the way they do business and, even though it does not intentionally do so, sometimes results in a loss of livelihood. The project manager always needs to keep the people side of the project in the forefront of his or her mind. Whether using the PDCA or DMAIC life cycle, people inside and outside a project's domain may be affected and can have a positive or negative impact on the performance of the Lean project. Identifying, communicating, and working with stakeholders are key responsibilities the project manager and the entire team need to understand and appreciate.

Train stakeholders. Often overlooked, training is important for people to participate in a Lean project. This training should include using tools, techniques, and concepts for both PM and process improvement. Through training, stakeholders use a common language; become more proficient in applying tools, techniques, and concepts; increase the opportunity for engagement; and enhance their skills and knowledge for use on future Lean projects. To leverage these benefits, training should occur as early as possible. One final point about training: it is a continuous process. Training occurs throughout the PDCA or DMAIC life cycle and people learn from experience as well as from the classroom, so to speak. "Experiential learning" serves as a means for moving a project forward, not backward, by recognizing what works and what does not work. The iterative characteristic of a Lean project allows for leveraging such experience.

Monitor performance throughout the Lean life cycle. The project should be monitored in several areas. One area is PM, which entails determining how well the project is performing according to the project baseline. The other area is process improvement, which entails looking, from a customer satisfaction perspective, at how well waste is being reduced or eliminated. What the two areas have in common is variation, that is, the difference between what is planned and what is actually occurring. Throughout the life cycle of a Lean project, attention is paid to identifying variation and determining its degree of significance. In some cases, the variation may be small, requiring little, if any, remedial action by the project team. In other cases, the variation may be significant enough that it requires taking a whole new approach, whether from a PM or process improvement perspective.

5.2 OVERVIEW OF PROJECT MANAGEMENT PROCESSES

There are six PM processes that are applicable to every project; what varies from project to project is their degree of application. These processes can be employed on Lean projects, too. These processes are defining, planning, organizing, executing, monitoring and controlling, and closing.

Defining is determining in advance the vision for the project. *Organizing* involves putting together the support infrastructure for the project. *Planning* is coming up with a road map to achieve the vision for the project. *Executing* is implementing the plans efficiently and effectively. *Monitoring and controlling* is determining how well a project is achieving the vision and whether any corrective actions are necessary. *Closing* is concluding a project.

All six processes work together to complete a project, whether Lean or some other type. Generally, defining comes first followed concurrently by organizing and planning which are, in turn, followed by two other con-current processes, executing and monitoring and controlling. Monitoring and controlling is followed by closing.

All processes occur for managing the entire life cycle of a Lean project. Within each phase, the same processes may occur for a phase. Take the following example for a PDCA project. The overall management of the project will have its own set of the PM processes to manage the entire life cycle. The plan phase of the PDCA cycle may also have its own PM processes; however, this application will depend on the scale and complexity of the project and also for the phase. The same concept applies to Lean projects using the DMAIC project, too.

Sometimes a seventh process is adopted that runs concurrently with all six other processes. Technically, it is not a process but serves as an effective enabler of the other processes. This process, if it can be accepted as one, is *leading*; and without it the other processes may not be as effective in their application. Leading is essentially motivating people to meet or exceed expectations by doing what is right for the project. Without leading, a project manager is simply managing, that is, going through the motions, so to speak, to apply the processes. With leading, the project manager applies the processes according to what is required rather than simply going through the motions. In other words, leading involves doing the right things and not just doing things right.

5.3 RELATIONSHIP TO LEAN

PM processes should work in concert with the PDCA and DMAIC life cycles (refer to Figure 5.1). They should mutually support one another. PM processes deal with managing the work of the project; the phases in a Lean life cycle are doing the technical work. Both must work together to develop a product or service that meets customer satisfaction. Good PM, without good technical output, will likely result in an unhappy customer; poor PM and good technical output will likely have the same result.

As mentioned earlier, PM processes occur not only for the entire project; they also occur for each phase of a Lean life cycle. This depends, of course, on the size and complexity of the project. If the size and complexity warrant it, not only do the six processes apply for the entire PDCA project, but also to each of the phases of the life cycle. In other words, defining,

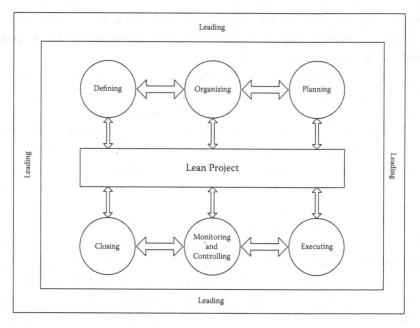

FIGURE 5.1
Relationship between Lean and project management processes.

organizing, planning, executing, monitoring and controlling, and closing can also be applied. The same is true for the do, check, and act phases of the life cycle. Again, the same pattern exists for DMAIC projects.

5.4 BENEFITS

The six PM processes offer several benefits.

Provides a structure for managing work. As a project grows in size and complexity so does the magnitude of work. A certain threshold exists whereby the lack of an adequate structure to complete a Lean project can result in difficulty in keeping a project under control and focusing on the vision. It becomes akin to dropping a multicolored bag of marbles on the floor and the contents scattering about. A similar situation can exist on a Lean project. For example, a multidisciplinary team can find its actions scattered about with some areas making progress while others fall behind. The goal is to harness this energy in a way that achieves the vision with the least amount of cost, effort, and waste. PM processes enable doing so by defining up front, providing a road map, establishing a supporting infrastructure, implementing the plan, collecting status, assessing performance, taking any necessary corrective actions, and bringing all work to a successful conclusion.

Focuses on results. PM processes all play a significant role in focusing on results simply because all subsequent planning and behaviors are directed toward achieving the vision, goals, and objectives. With the vision squarely in the minds of the key stakeholders, all decisions and actions are evaluated from the perspective of achieving it. If a change arises to any significant elements of a project, for example, charter or performance measurement baseline, stakeholders apply change management to assess the impact on achieving the vision. In some cases, the vision may need to change and the focus is on the revised revision; all subsequent decisions and actions are changed accordingly, which includes applying all PM processes.

Sets and manages expectations. Defining plays an important role in realizing this benefit. Defining provides an overall vision for a project, ideally replete with goals, objectives, and a scope. This definition occurs in concert with the key stakeholders, including, and perhaps most important, with the customer. All subsequent processes and technical efforts rely upon the vision, goals, objectives, and scope to deliver what the customer wants. Any changes, of course, must undergo change management to determine the impact on the vision, goals, objectives, and scope and to make adjustments accordingly, as a way to reset expectations.

Enables more effective and efficient use of resources. These resources cover labor and nonlabor, for example, time and money. Thanks to the output of the defining process, all subsequent phases entail using and assessing resources to maintain focus. Resources are employed with the purpose of achieving the vision, goals, and objectives. Additionally, during planning, techniques such as resource leveling and smoothing are employed to reduce inefficient and ineffective assignment of resources. During planning and executing, schedule compression techniques, such as fast tracking, can also be employed to accomplish similar results. Without these processes, resources, from energy to people, are wasted which can only result in customer dissatisfaction.

Encourages greater participation and ownership. Key stakeholder involvement is absolutely essential for the success of any project, let alone a Lean one. It becomes critical to share thoughts, ideas, information, data, and experiences among all stakeholders that everyone can leverage. It also becomes critical to share knowledge about areas that did not go well but, just as important, the negative risks that could arise and the positive risks that can potentially be realized. Through greater participation and ownership, resistance lessens because stakeholders who are engaged are less reluctant to criticize and reject something they had participated in creating or performing. Greater participation and ownership is achieved by involving key stakeholders when developing PM deliverables and practices. During planning, for example, key stakeholder involvement when developing a schedule can go a long way to achieve acceptance of the dates within it.

Encourages better communication. If ranked, in some respects, communication is the most important of all benefits. A failure in communication is a project heading for failure. Communication plays an instrumental role in defining by identifying, obtaining agreement or consensus, and informing all stakeholders about the vision, goals, and objectives for the project. It also plays an important role when preparing and distributing plans during planning, as well as establishing a supporting infrastructure during organizing. Communication is instrumental, too, while executing a project and monitoring and controlling to ensure that the project stays focused on its vision, goals, and objectives. It also plays a key role in closing to verify and validate that requirements have been met. As for leading, communicating is critical to motivate people to engage and perform at, or beyond, expectations. According to some institutions, project managers communicate 90% of their time. PM processes help them do that.

Engenders greater accountability. Each of the processes enables greater accountability on projects. Each process requires certain stakeholders to participate when developing deliverables. For example, to complete a charter for the defining process, the participation of key stakeholders, such as the executive sponsor and the customer, is necessary. The document also delineates roles and responsibilities at a high level. Planning also requires identifying roles and responsibilities in much greater detail when developing plans. Executing and monitoring and controlling, of course, help to ensure greater accountability when collecting and assessing status.

Provides an audit trail. For people who fear auditors, this one may not seem to be a benefit. Yet it is an important one. All of the PM processes require some form of documentation, whether in hard- or softcopy format. For example, defining requires creating a charter and a statement of work; organizing, such as forms and reports; planning, such as the work breakdown structure and schedules; executing, such as change management procedures and process, and revisions to the vision, goals, objectives, and requirements; monitoring and controlling, such as forms to capture status dates; and closing, such as a letter of acceptance from the customer. These documents, whether in electronic or hardcopy format, can be used to evaluate how well a project has been managed and led. It also can provide data and information in situations when litigious concerns arise.

5.5 CHALLENGES

As do all other projects, a Lean project faces challenges when applying PM processes.

Resistance toward PM. Despite evidence to the contrary, some stakeholders resist applying PM processes. This resistance may be overt, such as a lack of willingness to follow any PM plan, or with subterfuge, such as deliberately not providing timely accurate information. Resistance is often due to fear. It could be fear of losing independence. It could be fear of looking negative. It could be fear of losing one's position or job. It could be fear of being held accountable. Whatever the reason, this resistance can make it difficult to implement PM or to do so effectively. It is imperative that project managers seek the participation and engagement of stakeholders who may exhibit such perspectives, if for no other reason than to encourage ownership in the processes. It also may provide them the opportunity to suggest improvements when applying the process to enhance acceptance. Of course, some stakeholders may exhibit so much resistance that it may require elevating the issue to members of an executive steering committee, senior executive management, or an executive sponsor.

Not receiving enough training on the processes. Many people think they know PM and the relevant processes but when quizzed about the subject they display their ignorance. For example, some people think that a simple "to do" list is planning when in reality it serves no purpose from a time and resource utilization perspective. Other people think that merely beginning a project by simply talking with some stakeholders is enough to formulate a vision for a project; oftentimes that approach is woefully inadequate, leading to serious communication and expectations problems later on during the project life cycle. Others think PM involves simply putting out fires, running from one crisis to the next, when in reality they are functioning as an expeditor and not as a project manager. Without training on PM processes, such scenarios are all too commonplace and often assure project failure, not success. Training serves to increase people's awareness, knowledge, and expertise in PM processes, when performed adequately and in a timely manner. To preclude causing a host of future problems, this training should occur as early as possible in the life cycle of a project.

Not enough discipline and patience by stakeholders. Applying PM processes requires discipline and patience, both of which are few and far between in a business age that requires producing faster, better, and cheaper. The pressure can be immense for getting a product "out the door" and applying these processes with little or no forethought before proceeding. Lean projects are no different and, in fact, the more competitive the environment, the greater the pressure to not implement these processes effectively on a Lean project. Yet, key stakeholders need to sometimes call time out to think about what is occurring and to ascertain where the project is taking everyone. PM processes enable both to occur which requires discipline and patience. Naturally, applying the processes does not necessarily mean that all activity on a project must stop; however, it does require some discipline and patience from time to time to stop, look, and listen for at least a short while. Many projects, Lean and others, often move forward like a herd of buffalo over a cliff, generating a lot of energy and output that the customer does not want or desire. Repeat: key stakeholders need to exercise the necessary willpower to apply PM processes.

Viewing PM processes as "administrivia." Many people, especially people in highly technical fields, often see PM processes as nonproductive and burdensome. At best, they view it as a necessary evil and like all evils they are best to avoid for the most part. Not surprisingly, many stakeholders will work to circumvent the structure and discipline associated with PM processes. This behavior often persists even in the face of the great gains that have been attributed to applying PM processes. Key stakeholders need to insist up front that people take these processes seriously. This support needs to come not only from the top down but also from the bottom up, meaning that the stakeholders at all levels need to participate in determining the degree to which these processes are implemented and to adhere to that agreement.

Lacking sponsorship or support from senior management. The reality is that the tone often starts at the top. If senior leadership simply talks the talk but does not walk the talk for PM processes, then implementation will not occur, and if it does, then it will be tepid at best. Executive and senior management need to proclaim their support for applying PM disciplines.

They must demonstrate this support by expecting all projects, Lean or otherwise, to apply PM processes consistently and effectively. Frequently, Lean projects face the temptation to circumvent PM processes, either because some stakeholders feel that a process takes up too much time from getting the "real" work done or that the customer wants team members to deliver the product or service quickly and does not understand the implications of yielding to this pressure. The trouble with the latter is that the customer often gets shell-shocked over the costs associated with the rework, that the final product or service does not meet requirements, or that the project completion date continues to slide.

Not facing problems beneath the waterline. Unfortunately, not all problems are visible to stakeholders on a project. Many problems are like an iceberg floating in the Arctic; most of the iceberg floats under the surface of the water. These problems often arise at the worst possible time and may not become apparent early on from defining to closing. For example, the simple act of drafting a charter and encouraging discussion will bring forth problems whether people like the topics or not. The earlier such problems arise, the easier they are to address, especially less tangible ones such as political considerations and indecisiveness. Some stakeholders resist applying the PM processes to avoid conflict or to maintain the advantage or edge over other stakeholders.

5.6 GETTING STARTED

The following processes entail applying all the tools, techniques, and concepts discussed in the chapter on PM. Depending on the scale and visibility of a Lean project, the following should be addressed, differing only by a matter of degree.

5.7 DEFINING PROCESS

This process requires developing a project charter and statement of work for the overall project. The first deliverable should be a project charter that serves as an agreement among a limited number of key stakeholders, shown in Figure 5.2. The charter covers several topics and

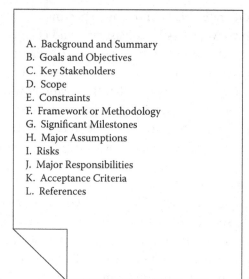

A. Background and Summary
B. Goals and Objectives
C. Key Stakeholders
D. Scope
E. Constraints
F. Framework or Methodology
G. Significant Milestones
H. Major Assumptions
I. Risks
J. Major Responsibilities
K. Acceptance Criteria
L. References

FIGURE 5.2
Project charter.

is restricted to two to three pages. The following topics are covered at a high level.

Background and summary. This section describes key information about the reasons for the Lean project. For example, it might describe the circumstances leading up to the problem or issue being addressed. It may also discuss the impact it has on the customer as well as on internal operations for providing services or a product. In addition, it provides a high-level statement about the purpose of a project.

Goals and objectives. A goal is a broad statement of intent, such as "to provide customer satisfaction." A goal, however, lacks specificity. An objective provides that missing specificity to achieve a goal, such as "to reduce the number of customer returns by 17% within two months." An objective can support multiple goals identified in a charter.

Key stakeholders. A key stakeholder is a person or organization having an interest in the outcome of your project. Key stakeholders often include a project sponsor or a steering committee; either one, or both, can provide oversight and resolve issues beyond what the project manager or the project team can handle. The sponsor or a representative of the steering committee prepares the charter. As often happens, however, the project manager may inherit the responsibility to prepare the charter.

Scope. The scope describes the boundaries of a project. This section describes the purview of a project. For example, instead of addressing a complex process or operation, it may describe a subset of an overall process or operation. This section also may describe what the project does not address, thereby identifying the exact scope via falsification.

Constraints. A constraint is something that limits options on a project. A constraint may be a limited number of available resources or having existing operations taking precedence over a project. Constraints often center on time, money, or other resources; however, sometimes these may include other topics, such as regulatory compliance.

Framework or methodology. How the project will be approached is described here. For example, it might include a methodology for approaching a project. From the perspective, it might describe the PDCA or DMAIC life cycle and some of the major deliverables resulting from each phase. It may also describe a specific approach used to produce each deliverable. This section focuses on identifying and describing briefly the framework or methodology used for both PM and process improvement.

Significant milestones. A milestone is an event that consumes no time or resources. The number of milestones presented should be limited to preclude producing a detailed schedule. Some examples of milestones include the beginning and end of a project as well as the end of each phase in the life cycle of a Lean project.

Major assumptions. It is important to capture assumptions up front and to revisit them periodically throughout the life cycle of a Lean project. Assumptions are treated as facts until proven otherwise, and they can have a big influence on the direction and approach for a project. An example of an assumption is dedicated continuous participation by the customer throughout the life cycle. Revisiting this assumption might involve periodically assessing how well this participation is occurring and its impact on a project.

Risks. These are something, such as an event, that potentially may occur in the future. It is important to identify, even based on a limited amount of knowledge what could potentially affect the performance of a project. Risk can be either positive, known as an opportunity, or negative, known as a threat. Often the focus is on threats. By identifying threats up front, especially the heavy hitters, the project can institute strategies to minimize or eliminate the impact if they occur. An example of a threat for a Lean project, for example, is a major stakeholder refusing to share information. An example of an opportunity might be leveraging improvements in a process for use in a project.

Major responsibilities. Delineating responsibilities occurs at a high level. The purpose is to help clarify who does what. Often this might be a listing known as RAAs (roles, accountabilities, and authorities). For example, this section might specify the need to involve the customer in each of the phases of the life cycle of a Lean project and the types of general decisions to make at discrete points in time.

Acceptance criteria. The charter provides a high-level listing of the criteria that the team must meet to complete a project successfully. These criteria often encompass both business and technical needs. An example of a business criterion is reducing overhead costs for a process by 33% or reducing cycle time by 20%. An example of a technical criterion is reducing weight of a deliverable by 25%.

References. This section cites internal and external documents and online sources to name a few. An example of an internal procedure is following specific steps to receive project approval of a Lean project costing more than one million dollars. An example of an external source is legal documentation specifying a specific procedure to follow that can constrain options for process improvement.

5.8 STATEMENT OF WORK

Frequently, but not necessarily, a statement of work (SOW) is appended to a charter.

Note: In some companies, a charter and a SOW have the same meaning; but for purposes here, these are treated as two distinctly separate deliverables.

The SOW essentially provides a more in-depth description of the work to perform on a project (refer to Figure 5.3). When complete, it serves as a basis for performing another action, planning. It also helps to define, in greater detail, what is and is not in scope.

The SOW covers several topics, some of which leverage from the contents of the project charter.

Overview. This section summarizes background information that has led to a Lean project. It usually provides a greater technical description of the work involved to solve the problem or to address an issue. Greater

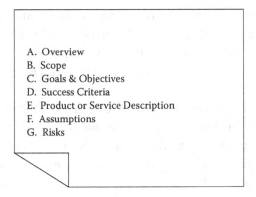

A. Overview
B. Scope
C. Goals & Objectives
D. Success Criteria
E. Product or Service Description
F. Assumptions
G. Risks

FIGURE 5.3
Statement of work.

emphasis is placed on defining the issue or problem that has led to a Lean project, as well as the relevant consequences of not doing anything.

Scope. It is important to describe carefully the scope of work that a Lean project will address. This scope will identify all or part of a process. The scope should describe the overall boundaries or parameters of the scope and its components and their relationships among one another. Also important is to identify subprocesses or procedures that are not part of a project. An example might be a critical financial process that is defined further into subprocesses, such as an accounts receivable process and accounts payable process.

Goals and objectives. The goals and objectives in the charter are further defined in greater detail, which will be used to plan the project. These goals and objectives are predicated on having a well-defined scope of work. Business and technical goals and objectives are all recorded.

Success criteria. The criteria serve as a means to determine whether the goals and objectives have been achieved both from verification and validation perspectives. Verification means that the solution complies with specific qualitative requirements. Validation means that the solution is found acceptable to the customer. An example of verification might be compliance with the Health Insurance Portability and Accountability Act (HIPAA). An example of validation might be reducing customer rejections of products by 33%.

Product or service description. This section describes in considerable detail the product or service to deliver to the customer. It usually describes the major functions or components and any performance needs or wants. It also describes how the different functions or components interact to meet the acceptance criteria defined by a customer. This section may describe in a narrative format, graphic format, or a combination of both. An example of a product or service description might show, in detail, the functions or components and their relationship with one another for a new accounts payable process and what performance needs or wants to satisfy.

Assumptions. The assumptions described in the charter are discussed in further detail in this section. Specifically, it describes the impact of assumptions on producing a product or service for a customer if they are not met, either from a business or technical perspective. An example of an assumption is that the customer provides a liaison to ensure that the requirements for a new accounts payable process are clearly articulated to the Lean project team.

Risks. This section discusses the business and technical risks that might affect a Lean project. Taken from the charter, the impact of each risk is assessed on the technical quality of the product or service being delivered. These risks may be opportunities or threats. An example of a threat might be a customer not providing the requirements needed to improve an accounts payable process.

With the charter and the SOW in place, the next step in a Lean project is to identify the requirements. Capturing the requirements involves identifying the needs and wants of the customer within the confines of the scope. In some cases, the requirements may be identified first and then the SOW. Regardless, the requirements provide the data and information necessary to begin work on improving an existing process. To a large extent, these requirements will likely be more clearly articulated during what is known as a kaizen workshop. However, a preliminary collection of requirements whether in narrative or graphic format can serve as aids during the kaizen workshop which occurs, for example, during the define phase of the PDCA cycle. These requirements will often be compiled from a host of sources, from existing documentation, data and information compilation, and interviews. The compilation should be well organized and approved by key stakeholders when presented at the kaizen workshop.

5.9 ORGANIZING

This process involves putting in place the support infrastructure for a project, existing as a significant part of a project office. Below is a description

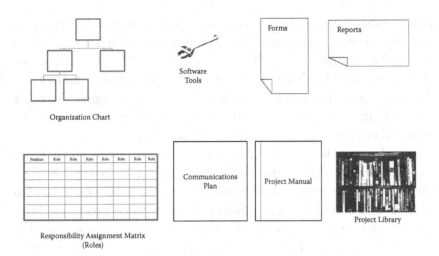

FIGURE 5.4
Organizing deliverables.

of the deliverables often put in place for a Lean project to apply the PDCA life cycle, also shown in Figure 5.4.

Roles, accountabilities, and authorities. More commonly known as RAAs, this deliverable describes the contributions of each different job category on a project. A generic title for all roles, such as a business process analyst, the general responsibilities for each one, and the power to make decisions under specific circumstances populates an RAA. The RAA serves as a guideline for assigning responsibilities, embedded in a responsibility assignment matrix, or RAM. The RAA covers all key stakeholders participating on a project.

Team organization. One of the other initial deliverables in the organizing process is to produce an organization chart. This chart will likely be incomplete until the planning process is complete. However, the organization chart can show the roles and reporting relationships among the actual members of a team and the generic positions that will eventually be filled. As people come on board their names populate the chart. The organization chart should reflect the steering committee, project sponsor, the project manager, team members, customer representatives, and other key stakeholders.

Forms and reports. Documentation, either in hard- or softcopy format, is important for many reasons. It serves as a repository of data and information that can be accessible throughout a Lean project. It serves as an audit trail to ascertain the source of problems, conduct performance reviews, or satisfy audit and legal requirements for evidence. Forms and reports are two ways to fulfill these needs. Forms capture the data and reports reflect conversion to information. When a project closes, these documents are then compiled and archived. Forms and reports prove their value by being defined up front and applied as soon as a Lean project begins. The key is to have forms and reports that are useful to stakeholders and do not waste time and other resources, especially on a Lean project.

Procedures and work flows. The project should have procedures describing the overall process for managing a Lean project. In some places these are called management plans. Regardless of the name, they describe what is needed to ensure that stakeholders follow common processes. These procedures often cover a wide range of topics on managing a project. They may vary in degree of formality and content. In some cases there may be a separate procedure for each topic; in other cases, only one procedure is necessary because the project is small enough. Common topics include change management, risk management, scheduling, issues management, resource management, communications, procurement management, and software tool application. Naturally, these procedures should be accessible to everyone.

Project manual. This PM deliverable is often overlooked. It contains a wealth of information that stakeholders can reference during the life cycle of a project. It contains a contact listing of key stakeholders, procedures, descriptions of forms and reports, communication management plan, status reporting requirements, RAAs, organization chart, and any other information deemed important to stakeholders. Every stakeholder should have a hardcopy but this may prove difficult to maintain. In today's technological environment, the manual can be stored online and everyone, using a common toolset, can access its contents.

Communication plan. This deliverable can be as simple as an electronic spreadsheet. It describes which stakeholders receive specific information as well as what meetings they should attend. Additional information might include agendas for meetings, contact information, and who receives what reports and the specific information contained within. The whole idea is to provide the right people with the right information in the right amount at the right time. Communication is absolutely critical for project success, whether for a Lean one or some other one. The communication management plan should be revisited throughout the life cycle of a Lean project inasmuch as stakeholders often change and the ones who remain may also have changing requirements.

Software tools. A Lean project has to be careful in selecting the right software tools. Some scheduling tools may prove too cumbersome for the scale and complexity of a project. Lean projects applying the PDCA life cycle often require less sophisticated software tools than ones following the DMAIC life cycle. A small Lean project can easily get stymied by a scheduling tool that requires considerable expertise to use and poses a challenge for interpreting the output. In some cases a simple spreadsheet and presentation software might suffice. The key is to use technology that supports, not drives, a project.

Project library. Like the project manual, this deliverable can be either in hardcopy or electronic format. This library serves as a repository of information that people can reference throughout the life cycle of a Lean project. The content may include technical documentation, reports, presentations, drawings, regulations, company policies and procedures, and any other content deemed useful for a project. Again, everyone should have the tools to access the content of the library to access it electronically.

5.10 PLANNING

Planning involves coming up with a road map to achieve the vision of a project as defined in the charter, SOW, and requirements. Several PM deliverables are produced during planning for the overall project (refer to Figure 5.5). The plans are further broken into greater detail for each phase in the PDCA cycle.

Work Breakdown Structure. Also known as the WBS, this deliverable becomes the ultimate scoping document for a Lean project. It is developed in a top-down perspective and shows the major phases of a project and the corresponding deliverables within each phase. The WBS serves as the hub to build the entire remaining planning deliverables, enable managing change, and tracking and monitoring performance. The WBS can be expanded for each phase during the life cycle of a Lean project.

Risk assessment. Some preliminary risks are usually identified in the project charter and they provide a good basis to conduct a comprehensive risk assessment. However, now that project managers know more about their projects, they can engage more stakeholders in developing a comprehensive risk assessment. Using the SOW and WBS, too, they can determine with some confidence the risks that their projects could face.

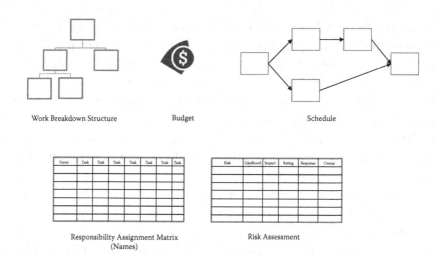

Name	Task	Task	Task	Task	Task	Task	Task

Responsibility Assignment Matrix
(Names)

Risk Assessment

FIGURE 5.5
Planning deliverables.

This risk assessment, in the end, provides a listing of risks as well as their priorities and impacts. For each significant risk, project managers identify strategic responses for dealing with each one. The results of the risk assessment provide invaluable data and information to make time and cost estimates as well as to determine the logic in a schedule.

Resource assignments. With the WBS built, the next PM deliverable is to assign responsibilities to activities for members of a project team. This action entails developing a high-level responsibility assignment matrix. A RAM is based upon the roles, accountabilities, and authorities defined during the organization process described earlier. The RAM at this point is useful to identify who provides time and cost estimates during the planning of each phase in the Lean project life cycle.

Schedule. This diagram shows the logical relationships of the elements within a WBS at the detail or work package level. The content can be rolled up into a milestone chart or bar chart. The contents of these schedules can also be expanded further for each of the phases if the entire project cannot be scheduled in detail up front This expansion will enable creating a network diagram that shows the relationships among work package levels and their activities within the WBS. Some milestones may have already been defined in the charter.

Budget. At this point in time, the budget was likely identified in the charter. The reliability of the estimate is questionable because the work has not been fully planned. As the planning becomes more refined during the entire life cycle of the project, a more reliable estimate of the budget may be made by stakeholders.

With the WBS, resource assignments, and the schedule done, the project budget can be finalized at a certain confidence level to form part of a performance measurement baseline.

5.11 EXECUTING PROCESS

During this process, the PM tools, techniques, and deliverables discussed in the previous sections are now applied. Two parts to this process exist: adhering to the PM processes and deliverables to begin improving a business or technical process (refer to Figure 5.6).

Operate according to plan. It is during this phase that implementing the project plan occurs. The relevant stakeholders should understand their responsibilities and the PM processes, procedures, and practices to follow. They should know what to do, when to do it, have an idea, and how to do the procedures. They also know the criteria for user acceptance. They should be very knowledgeable about the vision, goals, and objectives of the project. The charter should have captured much of this

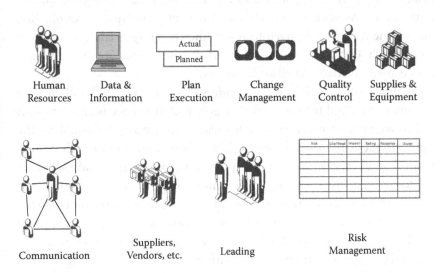

| Human Resources | Data & Information | Plan Execution | Change Management | Quality Control | Supplies & Equipment |

| Communication | Suppliers, Vendors, etc. | Leading | Risk Management |

FIGURE 5.6
Executing deliverables.

information as well as the statement of work, the WBS, and the proposed schedule.

Other actions can begin occurring during this phase of the Lean life cycle and throughout all the phases of the PDCA cycle. These actions include acquiring additional resources; capturing data and information; communicating with key stakeholders; complying with change management procedures; working with suppliers, vendors, consultants, and contractors; and managing and leading people.

Acquiring additional resources. Initially, a project starts off with a core team. The core team lays the groundwork to apply project management and produce deliverables. This team then determines at what point to bring in additional labor. As these resources arrive according to the plan, they may need to revisit estimates to accommodate their level of knowledge and expertise to perform any necessary activities. These activities are then applied while improving a process. For nonlabor resources, the core team accounts for any relevant lead times to ensure availability according to the schedule. If unavailable, then the team anticipates what contingency plans to invoke.

Capturing data and information. During all phases of a Lean project, data are captured, especially on the project performance and the deliverables produced. Data are converted into information for stakeholders as described in a communication management plan. All data are scrubbed before being converted into information to avoid tarnishing the quality of the latter. As stakeholders change, the content of the communication management plan is changed to reflect the changing needs and wants of new stakeholders. Naturally, the revised communication management plan is made available to all stakeholders.

Communicating with key stakeholders. This one is closely allied with capturing data and information. The only real difference is ensuring that stakeholders receive the right information in the right amount in the right format at the right time. Nothing can kill credibility with reports more than giving people too much data and information and their having to decipher the content. The communication management plan captures such information requirements, and all reports should adhere to the requirements captured in the communications management plan. Data and information can be provided both on a regular and ad hoc basis.

Another part of communicating with stakeholders is listening. A good communicator listens as well as talks. By listening, project managers can learn a good amount about what is occurring on their projects; they can hear what they need to hear, not what they want to hear. This feedback then allows project managers to make effective decisions as well as determine the source of a problem. They can then take appropriate corrective action. This activity requires listening to individuals and groups alike to gather a good perspective about where the project has been, where it is, and where it is going in the near and distant future.

Working with suppliers, vendors, consultants, and contractors. This action may or may not be relevant simply because many times process improvement projects occur in-house. However, external stakeholders may be brought on board due to their experience, knowledge, and expertise. Project managers need to work closely with these stakeholders because their actions and decisions may affect the final results when executing and completing a project. They can also influence the morale and esprit de corps of permanent stakeholders. A common occurrence is that sometimes external stakeholders participating on a Lean project generate suspicion among the rank and file, especially when the latter perceive that their positions are threatened. The tension can become quite intense under such circumstances, making it difficult for a project manager to manage and lead a project.

Adhering to change management. Change will occur and the longer the life cycle of a project the greater the opportunity for it to arise. Change can come from a variety of sources, including the government, the customer, or a team member. The key is to have a disciplined approach for addressing change to a process, product, and baseline. This means following an approach described in a change management plan. Changes should be assessed according to priority and impact and then handled accordingly, such as approving and scheduling it for implementation.

At all times, the project manager should make every effort to stop any attempt to subvert change management. Otherwise, scope creep can occur. Scope creep is the gradual expansion of the original vision for a project; it can dash customer and other key stakeholder expectations related to cost, schedule, and quality. Lean projects applying the PDCA cycle can help to keep scope in check by following a repetitive cycle.

Managing and leading a project. As mentioned earlier, managing a project is doing things right, that is, following what is expected in terms of procedures and practices. Building a WBS and a schedule are expected deliverables for managing a project. Leading a project is different; it is doing the right things. It requires making decisions that are not always popular but are necessary to further progress or deal with a negative conflict that no one wants to admit exists despite having deleterious effects on team performance. On Lean projects, whether employing the PDCA or DMAIC cycle, people issues often become very difficult. There are several reasons but the most common one is that process improvement generates fear because some people perceive that they might lose something of value, such as status, power, money, or a combination of all three. Whatever the reason, a project manager with good leadership skills must address problems early on, not later; otherwise, their impact will become apparent at the most inopportune times in a project life cycle, such as during the delivery of a product or service. In the end, it can, and more often than not, affect customer satisfaction.

Also important to leading is maintaining esprit de corps and morale on an individual and team level. Project managers need to identify and apply ways to keep team members motivated to progress through not just one phase of a Lean project but also through an entire life cycle. This responsibility becomes quite difficult in the face of negative conflict and setbacks that invariably accompany all projects. Lean ones using the PDCA life cycle are especially challenging in this regard because of the sometimes "porous" nature of these projects, meaning they use less rigor than the ones employing the DMAIC life cycle. The PDCA life cycle can be heavily oriented toward conflict if findings are mainly anecdotal and the recommendations rest upon subjective assessments. Sometimes this conflict can arise in a manner that appears irreconcilable and yet project managers must do their best to resolve such conflicts to conclude successfully.

Revisiting the risk assessment. Through all phases of the PDCA life cycle, project managers and other key stakeholders need to revisit the risks for their projects. This review includes risks, priorities, impacts, and strategies to ascertain relevancy and importance as well as the adequacy of planned and actual responses. Most projects happen in dynamic environments that present a changing list of risks and their attributes, for example, priority and impact. The assessment will likely also result in impacts on estimates on performing specific activities in a schedule which, in turn, require revisiting. After reassessing risks, the results should be communicated to key stakeholders.

Reviewing the quality of output. This activity is much more difficult than what many people think, especially with Lean projects. The ultimate arbiter is the customer because anything that does not achieve its goals is considered waste. Communicating with the customer and obtaining its engagement are two important ways to increase the likelihood to improve quality because of ongoing feedback. Additionally, quality is in the processes (not to be confused with the business process under review) involved when performing each phase of the Lean life cycle. Furthermore, quality is fulfilling what the customer wants, not exceeding expectations which only lead to scope creep. The fundamental challenge is that quality really is in the eye of the beholder, meaning in this case the customer, on Lean projects. This circumstance involves a subjective assessment by the customer, especially if the PDCA life cycle is employed.

5.12 MONITORING AND CONTROLLING

The monitoring and controlling of a Lean project occurs concurrently with executing. This PM process is analogous to a doctor checking the symptoms of a patient to determine health status and then deciding what action to take. Communication, as with other process groups is critical; however, it is absolutely essential if projects are to progress as planned and, if not, recognizing that a problem or issue exists and determining what action or actions are necessary to proceed according to plan in the future. Monitoring and controlling involves several actions to take in this regard. These actions are following PM procedures, collecting metrics, comparing planned and actual performance, analyzing and evaluating performance, taking remedial action, controlling procurements, and applying change management (as shown in Figure 5.7).

Following PM procedures. Following PM procedures is especially important during monitoring and controlling when collecting data and information about the performance of a Lean project. By following the procedures developed in the organizing process group, project managers can feel confident about their feedback. Obtaining this feedback is, however, easier said

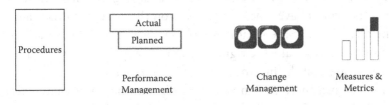

FIGURE 5.7
Monitoring and controlling deliverables.

than done, especially when executing a project. People may be focusing so much on their technical responsibilities, for example, that they may find collecting status as interfering with "real" work. Project managers need to be persistent and consistent when collecting facts and data about project performance. Being persistent requires using whatever means to collect status from stakeholders. Being persistent is not, as already mentioned, always popular; this is especially the case when some stakeholders fail to fulfill their responsibilities. Being consistent is collecting the necessary facts and data at regular intervals and in a format commonly known and understood by everyone. This, too, is not always popular among stakeholders if they feel that they have "higher" priorities. Still, it is important to execute relevant procedures developed during the organizing process group; otherwise, the result will likely be an incomplete and inaccurate assessment of project status. Unreliable status then creates a credibility gap not just in the reports but also with the project manager.

Following procedures using the PDCA cycle is frequently a challenge. The reason is that PM lite is often applied, meaning that PM is applied at a relatively high level. It is true that the rigor advocated by some professional associations for office-type environments can result in overkill and can actually be counterproductive. The procedures for collecting facts and data on performance are often at a high level and do not demand the rigor that is often associated with DMAIC projects. The tendency is simply to go with personal subjective assessments and mental estimates of percent complete without much regard to the reliability of these data and information. Procedures, too, are not often consistently followed due to the simplicity of the PDCA cycle. For small PDCA projects, this approach may suffice; but for medium to large projects PM lite may simply be a prescription to generate meaningless reports and, ultimately, result in project failure.

Generating metrics. Having the right data allows project managers to have reliable information to determine how well their projects are progressing. Without reliable facts and data project managers will likely make decisions that could have a negative impact on their project. It is important, therefore, to have the right measures in place that will generate the right information to make the right decisions. If any data are tainted the chances increase that the information will become suspect.

It is imperative, therefore, to provide sufficient measures that generate useful metrics. From a PM perspective, these metrics center on the performance measurement baseline, consisting of cost, schedule, and scope criteria. The keys to successful metrics are twofold. They tell a true story about the performance of a project, and they indicate whether corrective action is necessary. The former action is to determine what measures are required to generate the desired metrics. These measures should have meaning to stakeholders and should not be done simply to collect data to generate information that ultimately has no meaning to anyone. More is not better in this regard and, quite frankly, may be counterproductive. To do that requires ensuring that the data are reliable, meaning scrubbing them to remove inaccuracies and inconsistencies. Once scrubbing is complete, the latter action is to generate information in the form of metrics that are easy to understand, useful to the recipient, and that enable an accurate understanding of what was, is, and will be happening on a project. The information is presented in a format that satisfies the stakeholders who receive it; both stakeholders and content should be identified in the communication management plan.

For PDCA projects, these measures are often at a high level albeit not necessarily so. The level of depth regarding metrics depends on the size, visibility, and complexity of a project. It also depends on the stakeholders who will receive the output. The higher a project manager reports up the chain of command, it is best to produce summary metrics; the lower the chain of command the more detail is better as long as the content is relevant to the stakeholder doing the work.

When data is collected at a high level, the "alarm bells" should always be present, especially on PDCA projects. The tendency is to accept very subjective assessments that are riddled with ambiguity. As a heuristic, meaning a rule of thumb, it is better to strive for objectivity through numerical measures than accepting a subjective assessment. If subjective assessments are all that are available, as is often the case associated with PM lite, project managers must be prepared to question the responses when requesting data to ascertain reliability if they hope to assess the performance measurement baseline meaningfully. For instance, simple percent completes that are not based upon measurements are notoriously inaccurate, such as the perennial, "I am 95% complete." Skepticism is critical.

Comparing planned and actual performance. With reliable data and useful information, project managers can compare what is supposed to happen with what has actually happened and will happen if current levels of performance occur in the future. The idea here is to ascertain whether the project is progressing according to the plan agreed upon by all the key stakeholders. The metrics, which include cost, schedule, and scope data, should indicate whether progress is proceeding as expected. Whether for cost or schedule, for example, the differences between planned and actual may be different and the significance determined by the degree or magnitude of the variance, that is, the difference between planned and actual. In some cases, the variance may naturally recover before the next reporting period; in other cases, corrective action may be necessary to make appropriate changes. And, if that does not help, replanning, in whole or part, may have to occur.

For projects using the PDCA, comparing planned with actual performance is very difficult because PM lite is often applied, meaning the lack of rigor in tracking performance necessitates receiving more feedback from the people doing the work, which is good but too subjective. Project managers need to discuss and cross-check extensively to ensure that the data used for comparing planned versus actual performance are accurate and complete. Otherwise, the results will likely be unreliable and, therefore, provide little value to key stakeholders.

After comparing the planned and actual performance, project managers and other key stakeholders have to make a decision to continue with the current level of performance or take some remedial action, which is doing something that aligns actual performance with planned performance or replans the remainder of the project. The decision to replan should not be taken lightly because it requires slowing the momentum of a project and may consume resources and extend the timeline available for completion.

In many environments applying the PDCA cycle, a tendency exists not to develop cost and schedule baselines. Instead, the planned baselines get status but the dates continually move, leading to one slide after another. No baseline equals no discipline and makes it difficult to determine whether the performance metrics for a project will be met. If no performance measurement baseline exists, the impact of a failure to perform is difficult to determine and assess. The project manager will have to collect status continually in a reactive manner, reflected in constant revisions.

Applying change management. During monitoring and controlling, the metrics may reveal that a project is not progressing as expected. The cause could be due to one or more factors, such as an unrealistic schedule, an unanticipated technical problem, lack of information, or a change in managerial direction, and significant corrective action may be required.

Regardless of the type or degree of change, what is meant by "significant" should be defined by the PM plan or procedures. Usually a significant change involves some alteration to the performance measurement baseline, which includes cost, schedule, and scope. The corrective action under such conditions necessitates submitting the proposed action for approval or disapproval via integrated change control.

Because many Lean projects applying the PDCA cycle tend to embrace PM lite, a performance measurement baseline is often opaque at best, thereby making it extremely difficult to ascertain the cause for making a change and determining its impact. Under this circumstance, it behooves project managers to obtain a review and approval or disapproval from the project sponsor or steering committee. If the Lean project is substantial in terms of scope, for example, a formal change board may exist and the impact of a significant corrective action can then be assessed and subsequently approved or disapproved.

5.13 CLOSING

Closing is often the most overlooked process group in project management. More often than not, stakeholders are just happy the project is over, especially if it was extremely grueling. Nonetheless, there are some significant activities to conduct when closing a project. These are closing contracts, compiling and archiving data and information, verifying and validating the product or service, delivering the project or service to the customer, and conducting a lessons learned (shown in Figure 5.8).

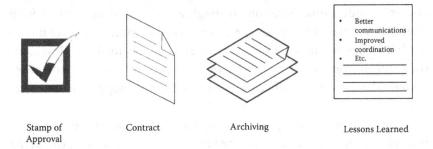

Stamp of Approval   Contract   Archiving   Lessons Learned

FIGURE 5.8
Closing deliverables.

Obtaining acceptance of the product or service. Upon completing a product or service for delivery, the customer must obviously review the output. The customer ensures that the product or service satisfies the requirements, such as the ones delineated in the statement of work. Sometimes, a requirements or specifications document provides greater detail than what appears in the SOW. Regardless, something equivalent to acceptance testing is conducted with the customer to ensure satisfaction with the product or service. Often this satisfaction must occur in two areas: the functional and performance requirements as defined by the customer and compliance with certain standards, such as one dealing with industry standards or the law. Sometimes, before acceptance testing occurs, the Lean team conducts its own tests to verify that requirements and standards have been met and, if so, then acceptance testing occurs.

For Lean projects applying the PDCA cycle, validating and verifying requirements and standards are often quite simple. The final assessment and decision rest with the customer. If the customer feels satisfied with the product or service, the project is over. The downside with Lean projects applying this principle is that the customer may never express its satisfaction and the project keeps going on and on with seemingly no end in sight.

Closing contracts. As a phase or project comes to a conclusion and the work has been found acceptable to the customer, all contractual obligations with vendors, suppliers, contractors, and consultants must come to an end. This action requires reviewing the terms and conditions to ascertain whether all obligations are complete on both sides. If the customer is satisfied, it makes little sense to keep the contract open; doing so will only add costs.

The challenge with Lean projects using the PDCA cycle is that it may take many additional iterations through a cycle before a contract with a vendor, supplier, consultant, or contractor can come to a close due to the life cycle's iterative nature. Still, every effort is made to close contracts when work is complete. This requires project managers and other stakeholders to watch costs closely when obtaining support from external parties.

Compiling and archiving data and information. If the customer is satisfied with the product or service, the project manager can start gathering data and information about the project. The data and information can be hard- and softcopies of documents and may include data stored in spreadsheets or repositories; correspondence, such as emails, financial agreements, accounts payable, and accounts receivable documentation; schedules; burndown and burnup charts; PM documentation; and other pertinent material. These data and information are indexed and archived for easy access. It should be accessible to project managers and other project professionals who will be involved with Lean projects of a similar nature. It should also be accessible to auditors to ascertain how PM and Lean were executed during the project. Finally, it should be accessible to lawyers and other legal experts if litigation should arise over any process improvements made that resulted in injuries to an internal or external stakeholder.

For Lean projects using the PDCA cycle, compiling and archiving data and information are not an issue. There is often plenty of material to handle. In fact, the challenge will be what information to exclude when compiling and archiving. The decision on what to include and exclude is often done by the project manager and project sponsor. Criteria for making such decisions are based upon the purpose and scope of a Lean project, the material used to determine improvements in a business process, any material used to make decisions to proceed with the project, and any material that significantly relates to the performance management baseline.

Conducting a lessons learned session. No project should conclude without a lessons learned session and a document that captures the feedback during that session. In fact, it is best to have a lessons learned session at the conclusion of each phase so that no feedback is lost due to turnover or memory loss. For example, a lessons learned session might be conducted right after completing each phase of a PDCA project. Once the project is complete, the lessons learned from each phase are compiled into one document.

What goes into a lessons learned document? A lessons learned consists of four sections. The first section provides background information about the project; it should be a high-level overview because more details reside in other project documentation, such as the charter. The second section describes what went well during the project and some of the contributing factors to the outcome; it may even identify some best practices. The third section describes what did not go so well and some contributing factors for the outcome. The fourth section describes any recommendations for improvement applicable to future projects of a similar nature.

5.14 FINAL INSIGHTS

PM processes are applicable and provide value to Lean projects. The data and findings by professional institutes and other organizations verify their effectiveness and their contributions to the efficiency of projects across all industries. Lean projects can especially benefit from PM processes because they provide a structure to manage the work performed regardless of whether applying the PDCA or DMAIC life cycle.

5.15 GETTING STARTED CHECKLIST

Question	Yes	No
1. For your Lean project, did you consider these key concepts: Define the Lean problem or issue as clearly as possible? Avoid being overly ambitious? Solicit and maintain customer involvement? Take a multi-functional approach? Identify all the relevant quality tools and techniques regardless of life cycle? Consistently apply the phases of the Lean life cycle? Involve key stakeholders throughout the Lean project? Determine the degree of project management to apply? Recognize the people side? Train stakeholders? Monitor performance throughout the Lean life cycle?		
2. For the project management processes, have you identified: The processes to employ? To what degree they will be applied for the entire project and, if relevant, for each phase in the Lean life cycle? The sequence of the processes?		
3. Have you realized the following benefits for employing the six project management processes? (If no, determine how to best realize the following benefits.): Provides a structure for managing work Focuses on results Sets and manages expectations Enables more effective and efficient use of resources Encourages greater participation and ownership Encourages better communications Engenders greater accountability Provides an audit trail		

Question	Yes	No
4. Have you experienced any of these challenges on your Lean project when applying the project management processes? (If yes, determine how to manage these challenges.): Resistance towards project management Not receiving enough training on the processes Not enough discipline and patience by stakeholders Viewing project management processes as "administrivia" Lacking sponsorship or support from senior management		
5. For the defining process, did you develop a charter that includes: Background and summary? Goals and objectives? Key stakeholders? Scope? Constraints? Framework or methodology? Significant milestones? Major assumptions? Risks? Major responsibilities? Acceptance criteria? References?		
6. For the defining process, did you develop a statement of work (SOW) that includes: Overview? Scope? Goals and objectives? Success criteria? Product or service description? Assumptions? Risks?		
7. For the organizing process, did you identify and implement: Roles, responsibilities, and authorities? Team organization? Forms and reports? Procedures and workflows? Project manual? Communications management plan? Software tools? Project library?		

Question	Yes	No
8. For the planning process, did you identify and implement: Work breakdown structure? Resource assignments? Schedule? Budget?		
9. For the executing process, did or are you performing these actions: Operate according to plan? Acquiring additional resources? Capturing data and information? Communicating with key stakeholders? Working with suppliers, vendors, consultants, and contractors? Adhering to change management? Managing and leading the project? Revisiting the risk assessment? Reviewing the quality of output?		
10. For the monitoring and controlling process, are you: Following project management procedures? Generating metrics? Comparing planned and actual performance? Applying change management?		
11. For the closing process, are you: Obtaining acceptance of the product or service? Closing contracts? Compiling and archiving data and information? Conducting lessons learned?		

6

Lean Project Management Using the PDCA Cycle

The PDCA (plan, do, check, act) cycle has been around for several decades and remains a popular tool to improve quality. It also serves as an excellent road map for performing Lean in an enterprise both as an overall framework and also as a specific tool to improve a process, procedure, or operation. This chapter presents the PDCA cycle from the perspective of the former. In some places, PDSA rather than PDCA is used, meaning plan, do, study, act.

6.1 PDCA CYCLE AND PROJECT MANAGEMENT BASICS

Perhaps the biggest strength of the PDCA cycle is its simplicity. Plan is determining the problem or issue to resolve and then building a road map to resolve it. Do is executing the plan. Check is measuring performance to determine if progress is meeting expectations. Act is analyzing the findings and making improvements. This cycle continues until a state of perfection is reached or when key stakeholders are satisfied with the results, thereby enabling pursuit of continuous improvement (shown in Figure 6.1).

Leading and all the project management processes apply to a Lean project using the PDCA cycle. They are applicable for the entire project and within each phase. At the overall project level the processes have a broad perspective. For example, a charter and high-level plans contain content at a summary or strategic perspective. At the phase level, the processes may amplify in greater detail the applicable content at the overall project level

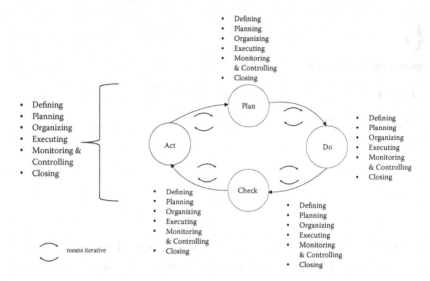

FIGURE 6.1
Project management processes for overall project and within each PDCA phase.

or, if necessary, be modified for the particular context in which a phase finds itself.

6.2 GOALS

Adopting the PDCA cycle has three fundamental goals. One is to provide a high-level framework for managing a Lean project. The four phases of plan, do, check, and act provide a simple structure that flows naturally and easily and offers sufficient flexibility for adapting to the environment. Two is to improve the quality of decisions regarding project performance. The simple transition from one phase to the next with reviews interspersed throughout and especially at the end of each phase increases the odds for success. Finally, it is to reduce the variability in outcomes in pursuit of satisfying the customer. The entire PDCA cycle, starting with the first phase, plan, focuses on satisfying the customer by solving a problem or issue related to Lean, for example, waste. All subsequent phases are predicated on what is identified during the Plan phase.

6.3 BENEFITS

Many benefits are attributed to using the PDCA cycle as a framework to manage a Lean project.

Easier and faster than DMAIC. The PDCA cycle, in comparison with the DMAIC life cycle, is much easier for people to handle. As noted earlier, DMAIC stands for define, measure, analyze, improve, and control. One reason for being easier and faster is that the DMAIC really is a combination of Six Sigma and Lean which requires considerable data collection and mathematical calculations not necessarily required under the PDCA cycle. However, keep in mind that the PDCA cycle does not preclude the use of considerable data collection and mathematical calculations; it's just that extensive data collection and mathematical calculations are not often associated with it to the extent of DMAIC. The PDCA cycle works best in an environment where speed is necessary to solve a problem or issue.

Familiarity. The PDCA cycle has been around for quite some time. Employees with some background in quality improvement are likely familiar with it to a certain degree. It was used extensively in the 1980s during the Total Quality Management, or TQM, Movement and when W. Edwards Deming was becoming a household name. The DMAIC cycle reflects a combination of Lean and Six Sigma in which the latter has received considerable press but its understanding is not as widespread.

Iterative. One of the redeeming values of the PDCA cycle is its iterative nature. It can be used to address a problem or issue and then require stepwise refinement as a project repeatedly progresses through the cycle. This iteration continues until key stakeholders reach a level of satisfaction that the problem or issue has been addressed. Kaizen is the fundamental principle behind the PDCA cycle that emphasizes the pursuit of perfection through continuous improvement. The number of iterations, of course, depends on the scale and complexity of the Lean project.

Less mathematical. For some people, perhaps for a good number of them, mathematics can be intimidating. Lean projects applying the PDCA cycle de-emphasize, not preclude, using mathematics, such as probability statistics, to come up with solutions to problems or issues. In fact, Lean projects using the PDCA cycle can involve little or no mathematics and still have meaningful results. Naturally, mathematics can make persuasion for changes easier and can demonstrate the value of one recommendation over another. However, not all recommendations require math. Keep in mind that if mathematics is necessary, it is important that the data are cleansed so as to avoid working with incorrect or useless data that are converted into information and ultimately used to make a decision. Hence, bad data equal bad information and potentially bad decisions. Also, make sure that everyone involved on the project team has a rudimentary understanding of statistics, such as mean, medium, mode, and standard deviation.

Shorter learning curve. Because the PDCA cycle requires less mathematics than the DMAIC life cycle people can pick up the concepts fairly easily. People can, with little training, understand the basics and then move forward in identifying, recommending, and making changes. This short learning curve, due to its conceptual simplicity, makes it ideal to apply Lean quickly, efficiently, and effectively. The training for the PDCA cycle is fairly straightforward and the knowledge transferable within a short period of time.

Applicable to all environments. One of the clear benefits of the PDCA cycle is its applicability to different industries. A Lean project in any environment can quickly apply the PDCA cycle. An insurance company can just as easily apply it in an office environment as well as a manufacturer of heavy machinery in its production facility. DMAIC is mainly applicable to the manufacturing environment albeit it can be used in other environments, too; DMAIC often requires a much greater understanding and rigor than the PDCA cycle which outside the manufacturing environment may be unnecessary.

Less time and effort to apply. This benefit ties closely with the PDCA cycle requiring a shorter learning curve and being less mathematical. The very simplicity of the PDCA cycle is easier to understand and apply than DMAIC and, as such, requires less time and effort to complete a Lean project, although it depends greatly on the complexity and length of the Lean project. The concepts behind the PDCA cycle are very comprehensible and easily applicable and, hence, its popularity over the DMAIC life cycle.

6.4 CHALLENGES

Despite its benefits, the PDCA cycle has its challenges.

Repeating the cycle. Projects by their very nature require a short life. Once the solution is implemented, a project is over. Using the PDCA cycle, however, requires using the cycle at least several times to ensure that a solution to a problem or issue is thorough, meaning it addresses the root cause and does so according to specific criteria. The tendency of some projects is to end and declare victory without much follow-up. Applying the PDCA cycle often requires a willingness to ensure that goals and objectives are met and done so effectively. The planning for such a project may require planning several iterations to ensure success.

Introducing bias. Because the PDCA cycle does not necessarily require mathematics to determine the cause and solution of a problem or issue, it can allow the opportunity for bias to affect people's judgment. This bias may come from individuals, peers, or superiors. The key, of course, is having the ability to determine whether bias is influencing judgment, to call it out, and to offset its influence. There are a number of tools and techniques to offset this bias. The first step, however, is at least to recognize that the potential for bias might be, or is, present.

Failing to question assumptions. Assumptions are closely intertwined with bias. Assumptions are accepted as facts until proven otherwise. The failure to question assumptions can lead to reliance on erroneous facts which, in turn, leads to ineffective decision making. Assumptions may not necessarily introduce bias if a person is willing to question them to ascertain relevancy or correctness and to then make changes accordingly. As with introducing bias, there are some ways to challenge them. The first step is a willingness to revisit assumptions.

Not relying on facts and data. As noted before, Alan Mullaly, formerly of Boeing and Ford, once said in several meetings with this author attending, that the facts and data will set you free. Once facts and data are collected and converted into information, the reality is that they set a person free from bias, erroneous assumptions, and just plain prejudices when conducting Lean projects. When using the PDCA cycle, collecting facts and data and converting both into information is the best route to freedom. Unfortunately, many times adopting the PDCA cycle is an excuse to avoid collecting facts and data and simply doing a preliminary or cursory review to determine a solution to a problem or issue. Just because a project adopts the PDCA cycle does not mean facts and data are unnecessary; it simply means a Lean project may not have to emphasize their collection and use. Sometimes the review of a current value stream can result in developing one that just at face value is more logical, efficient, and effective in reducing waste and satisfying the customer.

Taking shortcuts. Because the PDCA life cycle does not involve the rigor of DMAIC, the danger is that people on a Lean project will take shortcuts; that is, they will not perform one of the phases as thoroughly as the others or may even skip one. For example, the define phase may not be sufficiently articulated to define the real problem or issue but rather simply treat the symptoms. Or, the do or act phases are shortchanged because certain key stakeholders for a Lean project feel that it is unnecessary and too time consuming to plan anything; the pressure may be too intense and hence the do and check are not well thought out. Succumbing to such pressure can result in implementing a solution to a problem or issue that, quite frankly, ends up being ineffective or serves as a short-term fix. A good project plan is an effective way to deal with this challenge.

Not involving key stakeholders. Following the PDCA cycle may prove so easy or occur so quickly that key stakeholders may be overlooked or simply ignored until the Lean project comes up with one or more recommendations. It is not uncommon for Lean projects to whiz through a PDCA cycle without engaging key stakeholders partially or throughout the life cycle. The key to overcoming this challenge is to engage stakeholders during each of the phases, especially at the end of each one, such as in the form of a check point review or frequent status review meetings.

6.5 CASE STUDY

From a high-level perspective, the following case study is about applying PM processes throughout a PDCA life cycle and within each one of the phases.

The International Event Planning Company (IEPC) is a global holding that plans conferences, workshops, and other events. It consists of multiple divisions, one of which is the International Training Company Services (ITCS) with its headquarters located in Seattle, Washington. The company has a workforce of over 3,000 people and generates total revenues of about $3 billion per year. Its primary mission is to provide a wide array of training services to public and private companies around the world. These training services include, but are not limited to, defining, designing, developing, and deploying business management and technical training at all levels for private and public institutions. It also delivers certification training on management and information technology topics.

ITCS has a president who sits on the board of directors for IEPC. ITCS consists of four divisions, each led by a senior executive vice president and supporting business units. The four divisions are the:

- Instructional Definition and Design Division, with the overall mission to perform customer training needs assessments and to prepare training proposals
- Instructional Development Division, with the overall mission to prepare training materials
- Instructional Sales and Marketing Division, with the overall mission to solicit and maintain business opportunities as well as to provide customer support services
- Instructional Delivery Division, with the overall mission to provide training to affiliate customers

The two supporting business units that serve the entire company:

- Shared Services Group, with the overall mission to profit support services to each of the divisions, such as Information Technology and finance and accounting expertise
- Enterprise Services Group, with the overall mission to support senior executive leadership of ITCS

Together, all four divisions provide an entire package of services to affiliates across the globe. Each affiliate must use the services provided by the divisions. This requirement has caused a severe strain between the ITCS training company and most of its affiliates because of the increasing breakdown of communication and coordination among everyone in definition, design, development, and deployment of resources. Many affiliates find themselves sandwiched between the ITCS home office and their customers when services go awry.

Although ITCS has its corporate staff in Seattle, it has affiliate offices located across the globe. These affiliate offices are profit centers, responsible for their own profit and loss within the company, but they remain legally part of ITCS. Each affiliate has a liaison unit from the home office in Seattle that develops and delivers training to customers for each affiliate but reports, from a matrix perspective, to a sales and marketing manager located in:

- Beijing, China
- Cairo, Egypt

- George Town, Cayman Islands
- Johannesburg, South Africa
- London, England
- Los Angeles, United States
- Miami, United States
- New Delhi, India
- New York, United States
- Rome, Italy
- Santiago, Chile
- Seattle, United States
- Tokyo, Japan
- Washington, DC, United States

Over the past decade, ITCS has acquired a number of training and development companies located across the globe. Although these acquisitions have increased the expertise of the staff and enabled gaining access to markets where it originally had no presence, the result has been a complex organization structure and processes that led to a deteriorating quality of services delivered to the customers who, in this case, are the local presidents of each of the affiliates. As a result, several affiliates have experienced a sharp decline in cash flow and profitability along with ITCS. For example, the processes to define, design, develop, and deploy training, whether online or in the classroom, have deteriorated according to feedback from many of the affiliate offices. Recently, the affiliate in Santiago, Chile, legally severed its relationship with ITCS, becoming a "broker" in procuring training and development from different companies. The result was an immediate sharp decline in ITCS market share in South America.

The reasons behind this decline in performance are well known. As mentioned earlier, ITCS has become a maze of processes due to acquisitions, the processes to define, design, develop, and deploy education and training. Training and development that frequently occur fail to meet expectations set by the sales and marketing division. Instruction often partially meets the requirements of the attendees at in-house and public seminars and workshops. The material, such as handbooks, delivered to the instructors is often incomplete or has mismatching content, resulting in different versions being delivered to attendees at the same training session. In fact, some materials don't arrive at the training site in time for the seminar or workshop. Some instructors are not well versed about the topic that they teach and instructors are changed at the last minute despite customers having received assurance that the person mentioned will teach. Some seminars and workshops have been cancelled without prior notice to the attendees. These, and many other, problems have risen in number, too frequently, causing a strained relationship with affiliates and public and private customers alike. Consequently, profitability and market share are declining at a rapid rate.

The president, Wanda McFarland, appointed a steering committee to determine whether a true need exists for a project to identify and address the issues and concerns that many affiliates have expressed. The committee was to determine, first of all, whether a project was warranted based upon the results of a business case. The committee consisted of the vice presidents of each of the divisions plus shared services group and enterprise services. Here are the members:

- Nancy Wixman, vice president, definition and design
- Donna Fritolo, vice president, development division
- Jesus Marchiano, vice president, sales and marketing division
- David Kleinstein, vice president, delivery division
- Mary Rotoro, vice president, shared services group
- Sandy Alexander, vice president, enterprise services

The steering committee then performed the work necessary to determine whether to proceed with the project. Based upon its calculations and data and information provided by the shared services group, the steering committee agreed that a Lean project was necessary. The president then decided to be the executive sponsor for the project and directed the steering committee, chaired by Mary Rotoro, to prepare a charter, which was eventually approved.

The steering committee reviewed a select group of potential project managers and chose Harold Fitzwater from enterprise services to lead and manage the project. The steering committee then required each of its members to provide a core team member to support the project on a full-time basis. The members were:

- David Packart (definition and design)
- Inata Ditma (development division)
- Steve Posner (sales and marketing division)
- Cindy Sanderforder (delivery division)
- Mary McMartini (shared services group)

- Howard McCasel (enterprise services)

Fitzwater then held an offsite meeting with the project team. The team reviewed the business case and charter and then drafted these deliverables:

- Communication management plan
- Data repository structure and content
- Kaizen workshop preparation
- Organization chart
- Procedures and workflows on managing the project
- Roles, accountabilities, and authorities (RAAs)
- Selection of software tools
- Statement of work (SOW)

Fitzwater and the team also thought it was important to identify the stakeholders and their degree of influence on the project. The idea of customer seemed too vague and required greater refinement. Knowing exactly who the customer was would make it easier to define the criteria for success as well as identify meaningful requirements. Otherwise, the project team might do considerable work that, ultimately, would be of no value to whoever the customer might be. This stakeholder analysis was critical, too, because some customers might be more influential or important than others.

The stakeholder analysis was also important for identifying individuals and organizations who would need to participate more fully on the project team. Without their input, feedback, pushback, or resistance might arise from any work or recommendation affecting them.

The team agreed to criteria for identifying stakeholders. The criteria contained several elements: power, influence, degree of involvement, approval responsibilities, and position. This information was then captured in a log. The team used the log to identify future team members as well as participants in the upcoming kaizen workshop. The team also developed a set of rules for interacting with one another at meetings. These rules centered on two topics: meetings and consensus building.

With regard to meetings, the team established the following rules:

- Afford everyone the opportunity to speak.
- Clean the meeting room after every session.
- Come prepared.

- Distribute handouts prior to the meeting within a sufficient timeframe.
- Keep within the timeframe allotted to use the room.
- Provide and adhere to an agenda.
- Set up audiovisual equipment before the meeting begins.
- Silence electronic devices, preferably by turning them off if not needed for a meeting.
- Use active listening.

With regard to consensus building, the team adopted the following rules:

- Keep in mind the concept of UAS, meaning understanding, acceptance, and support.
- Focus on facts and data, not personality or physical attributes.
- If discord arises, apply timeout techniques, such as using a "parking lot" to record issues, problems, concerns, and the like to revisit later.
- If necessary, bring a topic to a vote for resolution by using approaches such as Nominal Group Technique (NGT) or the Delphi Technique.
- Keep the "big picture" in the forefront of meeting attendees.

Fitzwater, along with the core team, conducted a self-assessment of the level of understanding and knowledge about Lean. They decided that they were woefully lacking about the subject. Consequently, he budgeted time and money for everyone on the core team and other selected stakeholders to obtain training in Lean and related subjects, for example, PM. He decided, with the concurrence of the project sponsor, to have people attend on Lean. He then selected a person on the team to serve as a Lean focal point whereby that person shared knowledge about Lean with stakeholders not on the core team. This person was also responsible for keeping people abreast of interesting topics related to Lean, such as sending out articles or Web links on Lean concepts and techniques.

If only one person could attend a Lean seminar or workshop, that individual would perform what is known as cascade training. He or she would train others on the topic covered in the seminar or workshop. If anyone attended a Lean conference, he asked that the person prepare a trip report that everyone could read, whether in hard- or softcopy format, or attend a presentation.

Fitzwater set up a project office. The office consisted of three part-time employees from enterprise services: a planner, responsible for scheduling; an office administrator, for tasks such as taking minutes and preparing correspondence; and a data administrator, for collecting and verifying data and information before being incorporated in reports. Their services are also available to each of the subteams.

He then presented the deliverables to the steering committee for review. After a few suggestions for improvement, the steering committee approved the deliverables. Fitzwater then scheduled a kaizen workshop with the help of all the core team members.

The project team then determined requirements for the workshop. It decided that the workshop would be offsite and defined its goals, agenda, and roles and responsibilities. The team also decided that it would bring on board a scribe and a Lean expert to run the workshop.

Below are the topics listed in the agenda:

- Introductory remarks
- Charter review
- Current state and issues
- Future state and kaizens (improvements)
- Ideal state
- High-level RAM
- High-level milestone chart
- Lessons leaned
- Help needed
- Next steps
- Closing remarks

Taking the results of the kaizen workshop, which identified 25 kaizens, the team grouped them into these categories:

- Training needs analysis and design
- Development
- Sales and marketing
- Delivery
- Support

Within each category, each kaizen was assigned a priority: low (1 point), medium (2), high (3), and critical (4) as well as difficulty: low (1 point), medium (2), high (3), and critical (4). The two values of priority and difficulty were multiplied for each kaizen to determine the level of importance. Each kaizen was assigned eventually by the applicable subteam described in the next few paragraphs.

Fitzwater, based upon feedback from the executive sponsor, decided to establish subteams within the project, each with a team lead and representatives from each of the other subteams.

The PDCA cycle would follow what it called an evolutionary or agile release of the final work. Essentially, this approach meant that the first phase, plan, of the PDCA would proceed through stepwise refinement until all teams felt comfortable with the results. A gate review was headed and then the project could proceed into the second phase, do, and continue until desired results were achieved. The third phase, check, would do likewise, and then through the final phase, act.

Each subteam had the responsibility to develop a complete plan to address the problems and issues subsumed under their respective category; all content of the subteams' plans had to comply with the requirements identified at the project level. Using the output of the kaizen workshop, each subteam was responsible for creating a charter, SOW, WBS, schedule, risk assessment, and responsibility assignment matrices as well as provide weekly status during the overall project review meetings. The status report had to follow a standard format to ensure consistency of reporting which covered cost, schedule, risks, and quality metrics as well as an overall assessment for each project. Whenever any subteam fell behind expectations, they were expected to provide solutions to improve performance to recover or keep pace with expected performance. The weekly status report contained this information:

- Critical issues
- Help needed
- List of names, to include subteam leader and team members
- Performance metrics and assessments related to
  - Purpose of project with a short one- or two-sentence description
  - Quality
  - Risk
  - Schedule
  - Cost
- Weekly look-ahead

With the input from all key stakeholders, Fitzwater updated the plans for the overall project. This included updating the schedule, risk assessment, responsibility assignment matrices, charter, SOW, and project procedures. Naturally, any significant changes had to go before the steering committee for eventual approval.

With the aid of key stakeholders involved in the project, Fitzwater developed a high-level milestone chart which showed the major events that have to occur on the project. Phase gates were established at the end of each phase of the PDCA cycle and were reflected in the schedule; these phase gates served as check points to determine if the overall project should progress on to the next phase. At a phase gate meeting, each team presented its results as well as identified touch points with the other categories. Ultimately, each subteam presented its reviews and findings in a presentation at the phase gate review and sought approval to proceed to the next phase.

Additionally, Fitzwater and the core team members agreed upon an online repository to store data, information, and documentation for access and review by relevant stakeholders. This allowed members of one subteam, for example, to see and use the output of other subteams. This capability was especially important for capitalizing on the work of the other teams to preclude wasting time and effort.

Fitzwater consolidated the reports into one summary report, which he submitted to the executive sponsor and all the other members of the steering committee. The format, content, and distribution of the individual subteams and the overall project were all described in the communications management plan.

Before proceeding to the next relevant PDCA phase, the overall project plan and a summary of the subteams' plans were presented before the steering committee for review and approval. The steering committee granted its approval with some suggested minor changes that were made. All material was stored in the repository.

With the defining and planning PM processes completed, the entire project was ready to begin the executing PM process both at the project and subteam levels. Fitzwater and the executive sponsor decided that a kickoff meeting was necessary just prior to the execution of the project. This kickoff meeting had all the core team members present. There were several reasons to hold the kickoff meeting. One, it provided an opportunity for all key stakeholders to assemble at an offsite location to communicate and share knowledge and information with each other. Two, it provided Fitzwater with a venue to identify and address any major concerns up front so they could be dealt with as early as possible. Three, it afforded the opportunity to identify and prepare to act upon any potential showstoppers. Four, it provided a way to build esprit de corps early on among key stakeholders. Finally, it provided stakeholders with the opportunity to develop and understand the overall vision for the project. Here is the agenda for the kickoff meeting:

- Introductions
- Project review:
  - Charter
  - Statement of work
  - Cost
  - Schedule
  - Quality
  - Risk assessment
  - Roles and responsibilities
  - Critical issues
  - Project procedures
- Subteam reviews:
  - Statement of work
  - Cost
  - Schedule
  - Quality
  - Risk assessment
  - Roles and responsibilities
  - Critical issues
  - Project procedures
  - Help needed
  - Round robin
- Next steps

After the kickoff meeting, the project began the executing PM process. Each subteam had its own kickoff meeting and a series of working sessions to further define its purpose and approach for all the phases of the PDCA life cycle. Then, the subteam executed its responsibilities for the first phase of the PDCA cycle, plan. The subteam placed special emphasis on understanding each kaizen, defining exactly the problem or issue, and comprehending the criteria for success. Much of this information was acquired during the kaizen workshop; however, now was the time to iden-tify exactly what to address. Each team reviewed the current and future state diagrams.

During executing, each team conducted its internal weekly review prior to the overall weekly one. The subteam leader would collect status and, with the help of a staff member, enter the values collected into a software PM application. The subteam leader then took the information generated and conducted an internal team review every Tuesday before preparing the final report to the project manager and eventually to the steering committee. The report, along with the others, was reviewed at the project performance review every Thursday morning. Fitzwater would then take the information from the project review meeting, compile it, and give a summary presentation to the steering committee. All of this reporting, of course, was documented in the communications management plan.

To ensure reliable status derived from monitoring and controlling, Fitzwater was persistent and consistent when collecting status for the project. All team members were to collect status using the same approach and he insisted that all percent completes were derived based upon the remaining duration. All team members were also expected to collect data approximately at the same time and in the same format. No exception. He also made sure that all team members followed the same format in their report to him. This consistency and persistency resulted in reliable status reporting on cost, schedule, and quality performance. If status showed a significant slide in the performance metrics, he expected the project manager to have some proposals to improve performance so that actual progression would once again match planned progression by the next per-formance review.

As the planning phase came to a close, each of the subteams verified the completion of all activities as well as all deliverables meeting the criteria established by the customer.

Additionally, each subteam held a lessons learned session at the end of the phase. The session discussed what went well, what areas needed atten-tion, and recommendations for improvement. As with all other project information, the lessons learned were stored in the project repository.

Fitzwater also, prior to the gate review, conducted a lessons learned ses-sion for the entire project. The focus was on the project at large and also included a review of the lessons learned from the subteams to ascertain which insights were common to them all. Like the lessons learned for each subteam, these lessons learned were placed in the repository. The lessons learned session consisted of representatives from each of the subteams, the project sponsor, and selected key stakeholders.

With the plan phase of the PDCA cycle tentatively complete, the gate review was held. The purpose of the meeting was to determine whether to proceed to the next phase of the PDCA life cycle, do. All performance metrics were reviewed for accuracy as well as to address any quality issues that may have been overlooked. The steering committee determined that all expectations had been made and the project was granted permission to proceed to the next phase.

During the plan phase of the PDCA cycle, each subteam conducted a risk assessment regarding the applicable kaizens that they were assigned. Each risk was captured in a five-by-five chart that reflected both its likelihood of occurrence and impact on the project. The likelihood and impact were multiplied to derive a risk rating and that score was the value plotted in the chart. For each risk, a risk owner was assigned to monitor whether the risk was about to be, or had been, realized. Each risk deemed having a medium or high score had to have a risk strategy to address it and a corresponding action to implement the strategy. Risks that were assessed as having an impact beyond the purview of a subteam were elevated to the overall project risk assessment.

Also, once in a while a subteam during this phase was faced with whether to change the scope or to request a revision to the schedule that would affect the overall project timeline. The subteam had to submit a change request to the change board at the project level. The change board consisted of key stakeholders from each of the subteams and various members of the steering committee as well as selected individuals from the affiliates and from among a pool of subject matter experts. A committee of the change board did an impact analysis for each change request. The change board then decided whether to approve or disapprove the request for change.

At the conclusion of the plan phase, the project team and all subteams conducted the closing PM process. Each subteam conducted a lessons learned session. It also verified requirements and validated deliverables with the customer. The schedule was closed and a final status report completed for the phase and submitted to Fitzwater.

All the PM processes were employed by the subteams the same way during each phase of the PDCA life cycle according to project procedures. Only the content was different for all the PM deliverables produced by each subteam. Of course, each phase had its own set of deliverables to remove waste.

After Fitzwater gave his final report, the steering committee project declared the project a success for version 1. The project had completed all top priority kaizens and met customer expectations. Waste and cycle time had been reduced and untimely and unprepared delivery of seminars and workshops was becoming history. The project sponsor along with supporting signatures from the steering committee members provided all team members with letters of recognition and cash awards. An offsite party was held. One week later, the project team began work on the next release: addressing the kaizens of medium importance.

6.6 FINAL INSIGHTS

Lean projects employing the PDCA life cycle still require employing the PM processes on a project. These processes apply to the overall project; they can also apply, as we've seen in this case, during each phase of the PDCA life cycle. The degree of rigor depends on the size and complexity of a project. The decision as to what extent to apply these processes is also not a unilateral decision by the project manager; it is a collaborative decision, involving all key stakeholders. The key to success for Lean projects using the PDCA life cycle is to understand the context and then determine, in concert with other stakeholders, the degree to apply processes.

6.7 GETTING STARTED CHECKLIST

Question	Yes	No
1. For your Lean project using the PDCA cycle, do you face any of these challenges (and have a way to address them): Repeating the cycle endlessly? Introducing bias? Failing to question assumptions? Not relying on facts and data? Taking shortcuts? Not involving key stakeholders?		
2. When defining your project, do you consider the following: Organization mission statement? Steering committee membership? Project charter? Project sponsor? Statement of work?		
3. When organizing your project, do you consider the following: Communication management plan? Data repository structure and content? Organization chart? Procedures and workflows? Roles, accountabilities, and authorities (RAAs)? Software tools? Team meeting and their management? Self-assessment on level of knowledge about Lean? Reporting requirements?		
4. When planning your project, do you consider the following: Work Breakdown Structure? Detail and rollup schedules? One or multiple releases of the product or service? Risk assessment? Resource utilization? Time and cost estimating? Critical issues?		
5. When executing your project, do you consider the following: Kickoff meeting? Performance baselines? Change Management?		
6. When monitoring and closing your project, do you consider the following: Detail and summary performance metrics? Frequency of reporting? Change Management?		
7. When closing your project, do you consider the following: Lessons learned? Contract closure? Requirements verification? Customer validation? Data compilation and archiving? Team celebration?		

7

Project Management for a Lean Project Using DMAIC

DMAIC really made its appearance in the manufacturing environment representing a merger of sorts between Six Sigma at Motorola and Lean at Toyota. Today, the combination of the two merged into one approach commonly referred to as Lean Six Sigma. DMAIC capitalizes on this merger to enable projects to improve process performance for the customer.

7.1 BASICS OF DMAIC AND PROJECT MANAGEMENT

DMAIC consists of six stages:

D in DMAIC stands for *define*, which involves determining the problem or issue to address, building a business case and plan, as well as establishing an infrastructure for a project; the goals are to determine clearly what the customer wants, and preparing to manage and lead the project.

M stands for *measure*, which entails determining in greater detail the requirements: mapping the current process, collecting data, identifying critical inputs and outputs affecting the quality of the output, and pinpointing variations to performance. The goal is to generate a baseline for use in deriving improvements to address in a later phase.

A stands for *analyze*, which entails delving into data and process details to ascertain the cause or causes of problems and the degree of relationship between inputs to a process and the corresponding outputs; the goals are to acquire a greater understanding of the existing process and to determine the one or more root causes contributing to the problem or issue to address.

I stands for *improve* and involves identifying recommendations for improvement, selecting the most appropriate solution for reducing variation, and optimizing the process in question; the goals are to formulate a solution that solves the problem or issue the customer needs addressed.

C stands for *control*, and it entails ensuring that the newly revised process performs as expected and, if not, exercise contingencies if the process falls outside an expected range of variation; the goal is to apply ways to monitor process performance and to address any variation in the revised process.

Leading and all the project management processes apply to a Lean project using DMAIC. See Figure 7.1. They all apply to the entire project and within each stage. At the overall project level the processes have a broad perspective. For example, a charter and high-level plans contain content at a summary or strategic perspective. At the stage level, the processes may amplify in greater detail the applicable content at the overall project level or, if necessary, be modified for the particular context in which a stage finds itself.

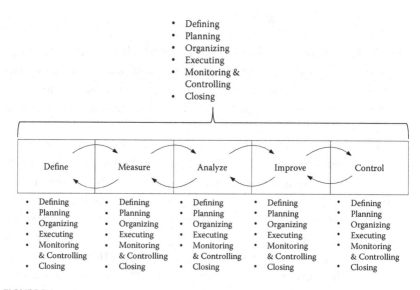

FIGURE 7.1

Project management processes for overall project and within each DMAIC stage.

7.2 GOAL

The ultimate goal of DMAIC is essentially the same as if applying the PDCA cycle: to satisfy the customer. The way to achieve that goal is to resolve a problem or issue to satisfy or delight a customer by removing waste that will increase efficiency, enhance effectiveness, and improve overall organizational performance on a continual, sustainable basis.

To achieve this goal, project management (PM) plays an instrumental role. The very same PM processes are just as relevant for DMAIC projects. Generally, projects using DMAIC, as opposed to PDCA, require a more in-depth application of the PM process because of the complexity and breadth of these projects. Regardless, however, the goals remain the same for DMAIC projects as they do for those using PDCA.

7.3 BENEFITS

Using DMAIC offers several benefits.

Emphasizes the quantitative over the qualitative. DMAIC places great stress on using numbers, rather than qualitative factors to understand a current process. This does not mean that the quantitative approach is more important than the qualitative. It simply means that the stress is on coming up with numerical data to understand what contributes to the problem or issue and how well the revised process will meet customer requirements. In other words, facts and data are absolutely critical for applying DMAIC. Largely, DMAIC requires subscribing to the old adage that what is measurable gets attention. This emphasis on the quantitative also serves as a more effective way to test assumptions and offset biases that interfere with coming up with meaningful recommendations. Facts and data can rarely be challenged other than in the way they were collected and interpreted.

Requires considerable rigor in the approach. For projects using DMAIC, the opportunity to skip over phases has a direct impact on the quality of the output of a project. If any phase is skipped, then the results in subsequent phases become quite apparent. The deliverables for the previous phase depend on the quality and existence of those from its predecessor, because the results calculated from one phase are used to compare with those of subsequent phases. For example, the calculated results about an existing process are compared to the ones from the improved process to ascertain if the latter actually resulted in changes increasing customer satisfaction. This rigor must occur, both on the technical and PM levels. Generally, the degree of PM also requires greater rigor in application. This greater application of PM processes not only occurs for the overall project but also for managing within each phase. Project managers are responsible for managing the work and leading the team to accomplish the goals and objectives identified in the project charter. They must coordinate with a large number and variety of stakeholders.

Stresses the importance of pinpointing the root cause. One of the significant efforts using DMAIC is to determine the critical elements causing the outputs of a process. Not all inputs in a process are equal when it comes to producing results. To make meaningful recommendations that result in effective change requires knowing the critical drivers, making the necessary changes to them, and coming up with expected results, that is, ones satisfying the customer. The goal here is to identify one or more meaningful improvements in a process rather than applying a Band-Aid that temporarily ameliorates the problem or issue. To a large extent, DMAIC reflects the scientific method whereby a hypothesis is formulated, a test is conducted, and the results studied to ascertain if expectations have been met. The fundamental difference is that, under DMAIC, one is conducting two tests: one for the baseline process to establish a standard and the other for a revised process to ascertain the effectiveness of a change. Then, if effective, the revised process is implemented and monitored. By addressing the root cause, therefore, change becomes meaningful and lasting unless significant variation occurs once again due to changing circumstances.

Places great value on definition. This definition comes at two levels. The first level is on defining the scope. From a project standpoint and from a Lean perspective, knowing the scope enables not only building a useful plan, it also enables focusing on efforts to collect data, identifying areas to study, and formulating meaningful recommendations. Too broad a scope causes waste in terms of applying resources and energies; too narrow a focus and the result may not provide any meaningful value to a customer. Defining the scope allows for meaningful technical analysis as well as applying PM effectively. The other level is operationalizing terms, such as speedy delivery or increasing customer satisfaction. All terminology requires sufficient tangible definitions that lend themselves to collecting data and conducting tests. By operationalizing, or defining, terms people can then better identify the "vital few" inputs and the resulting outputs rather than rely on assumptions that people view a term the same way. When testing occurs, it becomes easier to ascertain what inputs contribute to specific outputs and ascertain whether an improvement has met key performance expectations.

Puts the customer at the forefront. One of the great contributions of Lean is that improvement efforts focus on one strategic entity, namely the customer. The needs and wants of the customer become the reason for a process; anything in the process that fails to add value (short of some restrictions) to the customer is non-value-added. DMAIC requires that the needs and wants of the customer be the focus of a project. This focus on the needs and wants includes their identification, prioritization, and contribution to a process. The Lean project, applying the concept known as the voice of the customer (VOC), puts the customer at the forefront. VOC requires making every effort to understand the satisfiers and delighters of the customer; any shortcomings bothering them; their expectations surrounding quality, cost, and schedule; and then verifying and validating requirements. The customer is at the center of attention for a Lean project using DMAIC throughout the entire life cycle of the project. For example, it enables better scoping as well as generating a meaningful problem or opportunity statement. These requirements can then be applied to the product or service being delivered to ascertain which features or functions to improve, based upon the expectations of the customer.

Derives the solution, not imposes it. On many projects, the solution is dictated from higher-level management or by another organization. For Lean projects applying DMAIC, the opposite occurs. A solution arises based upon previous work performed in earlier phases. Understanding the current situation, knowing the needs of the customer, collecting data about the status quo, analyzing the information, developing solutions and selecting one, and testing it prior to implementation offer many additional benefits. There is greater buy-in and justification for a change, there is a solution that has been proven to work, and there is the solution that addresses one or more causes of a problem or issue. In other words, this approach helps to avoid an old saying, "Forcing a square peg in a round hole." If a solution arises that is a poor fit, it may in the long run create greater problems than what it was meant to address and will, more than likely, affect customer satisfaction.

Verifies and validates results. The power of measurement that DMAIC requires helps to determine whether technical standards and customer requirements have been met. *Verification* in this context is determining whether specific technical requirements have been met; *validation* is whether customer requirements have been met. In some circumstances, both may be in alignment with each other. In other circumstances, they may not. With meaningful measures using reliable data, verification and validation are possible with little or no threat of bias affecting perception. Without good measures and reliable data, verification and validation become a subjective assessment by key stakeholders. As with a camera, the information generated from the data using carefully designed metrics never lies. All too often, when metrics and data are missing or tarnished in some way, validation and assessment often reflect the opinion of certain stakeholders who, by virtue of their power or position, may necessarily not represent reality. Well-designed metrics can help offset this situation.

Combines data reliability and process efficiency. The use of the DMAIC life cycle depends on data. These data must be reliable, meaning free from inaccuracies, bias, duplication, and other threats to their validity. Process efficiency is how well a process executes its purpose with little or no waste. Data allow us to make that determination and also to formulate recommendations, such as reduced cycle time, that will satisfy the customer. In other words, data are used to assess how efficiently a process is working. The data, too, work hand in hand with effectiveness, meaning that the process achieves the goals and objectives of the customer. It becomes clear that data are akin to the blood cells that circulate through the body, analogous to a process. If the blood, or in this case, data, are tainted, they act like a poison, making it difficult to verify and validate behavior or performance. Therefore, it is imperative to understand the symbiotic relationship that binds data and process together when evaluating the latter's efficiency and effectiveness.

Asks the right questions before coming up with the right answer. This one is related to the other benefit: derive the solution, not impose it. One of the cardinal rules of problem resolution, in addition to listening, that is often violated is a failure to ask the right question or questions before developing a solution. Too often, just the opposite occurs; people come up with a solution before really understanding what the problem or issue is. The 1980s and 1990s philosophy of shoot first and aim later generated disasters in information technology; some organizations received technological solutions that failed to solve their problems or issues. DMAIC requires going into a serious review of the current process, identifying the real cause or causes, developing recommendations that will address problems or issues, and finally monitoring the effectiveness of the chosen recommendation. The chain that flows from the right questions down to the right answer has a direct link.

Monitors process performance. In theory, projects, by their very nature, deliver the product or service to the customer and end. The product or service moves, for example, into "sustaining and operations" as is often the case with information technology. Lean projects, using DMAIC, usually at least address the delivery of a product or service by providing metrics to assess first the effectiveness and efficiency of the revised process, and then to make any changes before deployment. Most of the metrics deal with detecting the degree of variance that occurs during the execution of a revised process. The point is DMAIC, particularly in the control phase, emphasizes monitoring performance once the product or service has been delivered. This monitoring enables keeping tabs on how well improvements are meeting the customer's expectations. Of course, the key to successful monitoring is collecting reliable facts and data to generate useful information.

Identifies what is and is not critical. The DMAIC cycle stresses the importance of identifying the critical elements of a process to make meaningful process changes. Special emphasis is on identifying the most important drivers for the outputs produced by a system. This identification is based upon collecting data and testing. Armed with those data and information, improvements can be made by altering the inputs and then comparing the results from the baseline and the revised process. There are three fundamental critical areas that are considered on a Lean project using DMAIC. Critical-to-quality (CTQ) consists of those requirements that relate to important functional outputs, critical-to-schedule (CTS) relates to timely delivery requirements, and critical-to-cost (CTC) relates to financial requirements. Knowing these and other critical requirements helps to determine what measures to establish to conduct a comparison between the baseline process and the revised one. Remember, one size does not fit all using DMAIC; the key is to use data collection and calculations to improve what are deemed important in a process.

Uses proven tools. This one applies whether using the PDCA cycle or DMAIC life cycle. However, it is especially emphasized when using DMAIC. Extensive data collection and information generation necessitate using a wide array of statistical methods and tools. In each stage of DMAIC, these methods and tools play a vital role for understanding, analyzing, and revising the baseline process to determine, validate, and verify the exact cause of a problem or issue and to then display that information in one or more ways, such as in a Pareto chart or trend chart. The same applies when coming up with a recommendation, making changes, and then verifying and validating results to ensure effectiveness in satisfying the customer's needs.

7.4 CHALLENGES

Despite all the above benefits, DMAIC presents several challenges to project managers. Some of these challenges also apply to the PDCA cycle. The only difference is they are often more acute in the DMAIC life cycle.

Obtaining data and information. This challenge is very difficult to surmount in some organizations where data and information are power. In these organizations, provisioning data and information can become a bargaining chip in negotiating for goals and objectives to achieve on a project. It can also be quite challenging when a downturn in the economy occurs and people begin to lose their jobs. Under such circumstances, protection and preservation become prevalent values. Much more than projects using the PDCA cycle, projects using DMAIC need hard data to perform statistical calculations to create a baseline of the current process, analyze the results, identify improvements, and determine their effectiveness. Data and information, therefore, are the lifeblood of these Lean projects. Any major restriction of access to data and information can affect change. This challenge can become augmented when proprietary data and information require sharing among not only employees but also contractors and consultants. To deal with this challenge, project managers need to know the organization's policies and procedures on accessing and sharing information. They may also need to solicit support from high-level management to grant their team this access. It is not uncommon on such projects to have team members sign a nondisclosure agreement before accessing and sharing of information can occur. As mentioned earlier, one of the keys to a successful Lean project is to entrust stakeholders with the data and information to help them succeed.

Narrowing down what is critical. There are two parts to this one. The first one deals with scoping. Scoping the process related to a problem or issue pinpoints the goals and objectives covered on a project and allows for developing meaningful tangible recommendations. The other part is using the scope to determine what the priorities for the project are. The term "vital few" is often used to describe those elements within a process deemed important to affect outputs. The idea is that by modifying the important inputs, improvements are identified and tested for anticipated results. These inputs can relate, for example, to cost, requirements, and time. With the scope narrowed, determining critical elements becomes less ambiguous, more recognizable, and tangible. Project managers have some important tools and techniques, of course, to manage this challenge. These tools and techniques include a project charter, a statement of work, and a work breakdown structure, as well as developing and implementing change management disciplines. They can also develop a table or matrix to reflect priorities assigned to requirements.

Overcoming resistance to change. With any change usually comes resistance. Some people will resist any improvement that does not further their interests. An improvement may be viewed as a threat, for example, to their position, power, or esteem. Sometimes this resistance is easy to foretell; sometimes it is not, because the resistance may not be obvious. Instead, it often manifests itself in subtle ways, such as political resistance, or through overt behavior, such as terminating support for a project just before completing one of the DMAIC stages. Project managers have several ways to address resistance to change. They can perform a stakeholder analysis, which will help them determine who has an interest, pro or con, in the outcome of their projects. They can form a core team of individuals consisting of representatives from various disciplines and organizations involved with the process. They can invite representatives from the different stakeholders to participate in performing the actual work. They can keep everyone informed according to the contents of a communication plan. They can continually communicate and coordinate with an executive steering committee for review of major activities and deliverables.

Defining the problem or issue. It is an axiom in systems analysis that 50% or more of solving a problem or issue is to know exactly what it is. In many cultures, especially those in the West, the emphasis is on coming up with a solution first; in the East, it is coming up with the question before determining the problem or issue. The latter makes good sense but the temptation is to go for the former. The only problem with determining the solution before really understanding or defining the problem or issue is that it may be the wrong solution and may actually worsen the problem or issue later. To a large extent, the reason for coming up with a solution first is that, in a world of fast delivery, not much time is available to define exactly the problem or issue. The result is often patchwork that never really addresses the problem or issue. Lean, especially when applying DMAIC, delays formulating a solution by first emphasizing the need to define a problem or issue. However, even using DMAIC is no guarantee, because immense pressure is placed on stakeholders to push the Lean project along as quickly as possible to focus on productivity and, ironically, reduce overhead costs (which is the purpose of Lean in the first place). Project managers must be assertive when dealing with this challenge. They need to insist that people follow all the stages of DMAIC and do so in a way that does not subvert the purpose of one of its stages. Project managers also have the ability to meet with their sponsor, steering committee, or customer to obtain agreement on what the exact problem or issue is and then to ensure that it is documented and signed off in the project charter, statement of work, or both. Any expansion of the problem or issue can also go before a change board for review and determination of whether any request or proposed action goes beyond the original definition of the problem or issue.

Abandoning biases and unfounded assumptions. On any project, biases and assumptions will exist and are often assumed as fact until proven otherwise. Even in the face of data and alternative facts, however, some people still adhere to biases and assumptions. Some people find it very difficult to shed their biases and assumptions due to their own paradigm, or view of how the world works. In fact, these biases and assumptions can be so strong that they can enable a person to foolishly ignore contrary facts and data; this phenomenon can occur on individual or group levels. Such rigid adherence to biases and assumptions can cause stakeholders to overlook viable recommendations to improve a process, or can result in adopting a recommendation that results in a greater problem. Project managers have at their disposal many ways to address this problem. They can bring on board outside stakeholders, such as consultants, to challenge biases and assumptions, adopt techniques such as brainstorming and the Delphi technique, perform benchmarking, review lessons learned of projects of a similar nature, conduct lessons learned, and occasionally change the membership of their team to offset the psychological and sociological pressures to conform.

Finding qualified and knowledgeable people. When the economy is bad, this challenge is usually not a problem. When the economy gets better and expands, it becomes a significant problem. Improving a process in a technological environment often involves many people with unique skill sets and backgrounds, both at a strategic and operational level. On Lean projects employing DMAIC, these people require certain unique skill sets. For example, these projects require some people to be Master Black Belts or Black Belts whereas others are known as Green Belts. Master Black Belts are people who have considerable experience in Lean Six Sigma and often support one or more Lean projects. Black Belts provide full-time support to a project and have some of the many skills and background of the Master Black Belt. The Green Belts are people who provide part-time support to a Lean project in the form of a specific expertise. Master Black Belts and Black Belts are project managers, the former being more of a coach or consultant. Both are knowledgeable in Lean Six Sigma and PM. One other group of people yet to be mentioned is the champions. These are usually senior people in an organization who embrace and further the mindset of Lean and ensure that the relevant tools and techniques are employed on projects. Champions are usually members of an oversight team, such as a steering committee, at different levels of an organization. One of their principal roles is to ensure that all Lean projects are successful by providing the necessary guidance and support. To increase the probability for success, project managers need to ensure that they, and the other stakeholders, have this top-level support. The support may be tangible, such as financial backing for the project, or intangible, such as providing the political muscle to overcome resistance. Project managers have the project charter, tool gates (also referred to as check points or gate reviews), and approval of deliverables. Above all, project managers, in this case Master Black Belts and Black Belts, need champions to provide them with Green Belt support.

Giving people sufficient time to support the project. This one is significant in organizations having a matrix structure, meaning people come from a functional organization and support multiple projects. The matrix structure offers several advantages, including making people with rare skills available and flexible in assignments; however, it can also be very difficult on people, such as working extensive overtime, having conflicting priorities, and supporting, although not formally, multiple superiors as well as projects. For Black Belt project managers this situation is not as acute because they support, in theory, only one project. For people who serve in a Green Belt role, they can find themselves stretched thin in terms of the support provided to more than one Lean project. If not managed correctly, the gains of working in a matrix environment can be offset by the negative consequences. Project managers of Lean projects using DMAIC can find that the matrix environment can extend their schedules, cost more, and deteriorate the quality of output. Nevertheless, project managers have several tools and techniques to offset this challenge. They can ask the steering committee and the sponsor to set priorities among projects that may have been done already if portfolio management has been implemented. They can perform leveling and smoothing to ensure that resources reflect resource constraints. They can appeal to a change board or steering committee to reduce the scope. They can outsource some work. They can negotiate with functional managers and other project managers to determine the availability of people to support the project.

Transferring to operations. Once the Lean project using DMAIC comes up with a recommendation and implements it, a time period will exist that still requires the people to adjust to a revised process. Even when a revised process makes sense, many people have a difficult time changing their perspectives and their ways of doing business. Because a Lean project does not necessarily involve all the stakeholders affected by a change, especially in large organizations, this adjustment period will take some time and will be difficult. Project managers of Lean projects using DMAIC, of course, have some control over this during the control stage and can help smooth the transition through training, producing procedures, and establishing metrics to populate a dashboard. Project managers can also keep the affected people of a process apprised of the progress to date by distributing information as defined in the communications plan. Finally, they can incorporate the training of people in the schedule prior to deploying the revised process on a full scale.

Inculcating accountability. Process improvement, especially for processes that span multiple organizations, can involve a large number of stakeholders. Some stakeholders have a greater impact than others. The challenge is to determine which stakeholders have a more significant role and to ensure that they produce according to expectations. It is not uncommon for people, especially in large organizations, to attend project meetings simply out of interest and sit on the sidelines and then take credit if the results are successful. Project managers need to ensure that such people are identified, do not interfere on their projects, and avoid incurring needless costs. They can handle this challenge in several ways. They can perform a stakeholder analysis to ascertain which ones have a salient interest in the project; identify roles, responsibilities, and authorities; assign people to specific activities; and publish a communications plan that restricts who attends specific meetings and receives specific information. Nothing can impede performance more than having people involved who have no accountability in a project's outcome.

Resolving differences. Lean projects, because of their often cross-functional nature, may involve many different people. They involve people at all levels of an organization, from the strategic to the operational. They involve people from different disciplines. They even involve people with different psychological profiles, for example, thinking styles. Projects using the DMAIC life cycle especially use a diverse group of people. Naturally, this situation lays the groundwork for conflict. Conflicts can be positive, and often are, but they can also be negative. If not handled appropriately, conflicts can hurt the overall performance of the projects. In the middle of all conflicts is one person who must bridge the gap: the project manager. This person is really the only one who interacts with everyone to a certain degree and this provides him or her with the opportunity to see all perspectives. If handled correctly, conflict can become the springboard for moving a project forward. If handled poorly, it can stop a project dead, and, under certain circumstances, the project manager receives the blame. Project managers have several tools and techniques to help them deal with conflict. They can always appeal to the steering committee or project sponsor to deal with the conflict, but that is often perceived as being weak and ineffective. They can take the initiative by taking other courses of action, including having a well-written statement of work and requirements document, having people participate in developing the work breakdown structure and schedule that will cause conflict to come out in the open early on, establishing rules for meetings that include agreed-upon approaches to resolve conflict, and performing a risk assessment early on to raise potential areas where conflict can result if a risk is realized.

Following the stages. Lean projects using DMAIC require discipline when adhering to its stages and in their sequence. As with most projects, a tendency exists to cut corners, especially if a project starts to fall behind schedule, exceeds cost estimates, or people feel like they are no longer enjoying the experience for a multitude of reasons. Under such circumstances, it is not uncommon for people to pursue the line of least resistance by short-changing DMAIC activities. The consequences are that the recommendation implemented does not satisfactorily address the problem or issue, which ultimately fails to satisfy the customer. Project managers can manage this challenge by placing a work breakdown structure under configuration management and requiring any changes to go through change control. They can incorporate gate reviews or tollgates in the schedule.

They can require peer reviews of output produced by key stakeholders to ensure that the right statistical method or tool is being used. They can also cross-check all output of each stage to ensure consistency with what was produced in a previous stage.

Lacking understanding and knowledge about DMAIC. Not everyone on a project will have a Black Belt or even have experience with Lean or Six Sigma. If fact, chances are that most of the people will lack knowledge and understanding of the topics. Chances will also exist that some stakeholders will think they are experts on these subjects even without any experience or substantive understanding or knowledge. Under such conditions, miscommunication and misunderstandings can be prevalent, resulting in negative conflict that can further result in an impasse in moving a project forward. Project managers have several options to address this challenge. For example, they can have all stakeholders attend an introductory seminar or workshop on Lean Six Sigma or one focused on DMAIC. They can send only certain members of the team who, in turn, train the other stakeholders; this approach is often referred to as cascade training. They can provide alternative resources of information such as online training sites. They can have the Master Black Belt provide the necessary training at the worksite. The key is to have training that is relevant to the stakeholders so they can participate meaningfully on a project. The training may provide a general overview, for instance, for part-time stakeholders, or it could cover specific statistical techniques.

Selecting the right candidate projects. Just about every process or operation within an organization can benefit from using DMAIC. However, there is only a finite amount of resources, from time to energy, that can be devoted to Lean. An organization still has to carry out its current mission, goals, and objectives. It is important, therefore, to select the right project or projects to improve a process using DMAIC. If the project is the first Lean project and a candidate to use DMAIC, the process being improved should not be overly complex nor should it be too simple. The process should have enough impact on the bottom line so people can see and appreciate the difference between the old and new way of doing business. It should have enough complexity to cause people to stretch and certainly give them enough time to increase their understanding and knowledge of Lean and the process to revise. As in any project selection, the goal is to choose a project that can demonstrate value to the customer while simultaneously allowing people to master new knowledge and skills. Building upon one successful project after another is the quickest way to encourage additional Lean projects in the future, each with increasing scope and complexity. Project managers usually receive projects after an executive committee, such as a steering committee, reviews and approves a list of projects. They can also review the lessons learned of previous projects of a similar nature, to see if any potential projects can evolve from that information.

Focusing on the short term. It is hoped that using DMAIC will help overcome this challenge. DMAIC requires identifying the source of a problem or issue by rigorously identifying and examining facts and data. If the team and other key stakeholders truly want to address the root cause or causes, they must not only proceed sequentially from one stage to another but also execute each one diligently. In today's environment, the pressure is to move with velocity, that is, speed and direction. Some of the work required to perform a Lean project using DMAIC takes considerable time and effort. Not surprisingly, some people may succumb to this pressure and gloss over some necessary work. The consequence is that a team may be recommending a fix rather than a lasting change. Project managers must encourage key stakeholders to take and maintain a strategic view of their projects. They should continuously remind all stakeholders of the vision, goals, and objectives of their projects that are, one hopes, captured in the project charter and statements of work; they can do that by displaying the vision, goals, and objectives at the beginning of each meeting, such as status review meetings, at kaizen workshops, or any other team meeting, for that matter. They should develop the work breakdown structures predicated on the information in a project charter, statement of work, and the requirements documentation. They can then use the elements in the work breakdown structure to build plans that ensure work is not glossed over simply to succumb to pressure to just "get it done." Yielding to such pressure only breeds mediocre results, at best, and may actually lead to greater customer dissatisfaction.

Creating a sense of urgency. This challenge may seem like a contradiction from focusing on the short term. However, this one deals with a different context. The concern here is that some stakeholders may view a Lean project using the DMAIC as an additional workload to address, if time permits. This perception can have dire consequences for a Lean project. For one, people will tend to view the project as having a lower priority than other responsibilities and, therefore, fail to give it their attention; people in operations or production often subscribe to this view. It then becomes a considerable challenge for the project manager to coordinate activities or to set up necessary meetings at a time that accommodates the needs of the project and those of individual stakeholders. Consequently, the flow time of the project tends to expand farther than necessary, and the project manager faces a serious obstacle in keeping people motivated and engaged. Fortunately, project managers have some ways to deal with this problem: they can emphasize the need to meet specific milestones as determined by executive leadership. They can have participants perform many planning activities that affect them, such as determining the percentage of their time working on an activity or the number of time units to work on, or the start and finish dates for each one. By encouraging participation in planning, project managers can increase the likelihood that stakeholders will get a greater sense of ownership and commitment to complete their responsibilities. As plans come to completion, project managers can give as much visibility as possible to progress, to include the names of persons responsible to complete upcoming activities. The intranet places considerable power in the hands of project managers in this regard. Another technique to create a sense of urgency is presenting only the current start and finish dates and not the two sets of early and late dates and positive total float. If people know that they have time to slide an activity they will likely do so up to the time available for its completion. Project managers can also shorten the calendar time between status collection and review sessions. Finally, they can, as a last resort, conduct daily stand-up sessions. During these sessions, each stakeholder with current and immediately forthcoming responsibilities on the team briefly discusses for one or two minutes what he accomplished the previous day and what he expects to do during the current day. He may mention any problems experienced but the session is not the time and place to problem solve.

Achieving simplicity. One of the biggest ironies of Lean projects using DMAIC is that the pursuit of eliminating waste through simplification can result in people making things way too complex. Many stakeholders start finding themselves getting tangled up in the details, sometimes forgetting that the whole purpose is to remove complexity in a process. For instance, some stakeholders find it very difficult to think at a higher strategic level because they treat all details as equal. Some individuals start to squabble over those details and more time is spent trying to formulate a compromise than coming up with a simplified solution. Or some people get so involved in the calculations that precision becomes more important than looking for patterns of behavior in a process. The key, of course, is having a strategic perspective in alignment with the collection of details in a way that produces a simplified recommendation. At some point, more charts, calculations, and data oftentimes reach a threshold and their value diminishes and only adds confusion. Project managers have several options at their disposal to deal with this circumstance. They can conduct peer reviews of the work done by colleagues. They can, with input from the team, set standards for deliverables. They can limit the time available to complete certain activities. They can select team members who, when combined, reflect many different mental models, thereby offsetting the tendency of groupthink or people with a certain mental model commandeering the project.

Defining terminology. In a multidisciplinary environment, such as a manufacturing one, jargon can become commonplace. For example, one group of people thinks a term means something when another interprets it differently. In the beginning of a Lean project using DMAIC, people start using terminology, such as a customer and satisfaction (or customer satisfaction), thinking that everyone has the same meaning or connotation for the terms. As the project progresses, it soon becomes apparent that some people have a different interpretation of just what these terms mean. This situation can result in considerable rework as the project progresses from one stage to another, all because of misinterpreting terminology. It can also result in negative conflict among stakeholders, thanks in large part to miscommunication and misinterpretation. It is very important, therefore, for project managers to operationalize, or define, terminology on these projects up front to minimize problems. One of the most important deliverables for such projects is to produce a common glossary that people can reference during analysis and formulating recommendations.

Obtaining customer feedback. Another irony of Lean projects in general and ones using DMAIC is the tendency to lose focus on the customer. Some people become enamored more with the tools and techniques of Lean Six Sigma, for example, forgetting about focusing on the interests of the customer. Unless the customer participates in each of the stages of DMAIC, this tendency begins to manifest itself more and more. This lack of customer focus can cause a loss of feedback. Of course, both could share responsibilities in this circumstance. The customer can contribute to this failure by sending liaisons to the project who really don't understand its needs. It may also not provide the time or data needed to perform a meaningful analysis or to formulate value-added recommendations. The fault, in other words, can be the result of the behavior by the project team or the customer. Project managers can surmount this problem by preparing a communications plan that encourages customer input and feedback. They can also engage customers in the planning of the project by assigning activities in the schedule. They can hold periodic meetings with the customer to obtain feedback; they can have customers attend status review meetings.

Ensuring visibility of performance. Some stakeholders like to operate "under the radar." In other words, they do not want any visibility of the work performed unless, of course, it has a very positive outcome. Not surprisingly, some stakeholders, therefore, are very reticent and hesitant in providing any status or communicating what they've done on a Lean project. They may not want visibility for many reasons. They may just prefer to work in the background. They may fear reprisal for not performing according to expectations. They may not want to associate themselves with the project directly in any way. They may not agree with participating on a project but have been told to do so. Whatever the reason, some stakeholders want to keep visibility to a minimum. The consequences are many, including an inability to collect and evaluate status for members of a project and other stakeholders, such as the project sponsor and steering committee. Project managers, when dealing with stakeholders who eschew visibility, must be assertive in the relationships. They have various ways to deal with this challenge. They can set up standards to report status, create a dashboard that lists stakeholders not cooperating in this regard, have reluctant stakeholders participate directly at status review meetings, and, ultimately, raise the issue to the project sponsor or the steering committee. Some negative approaches include sending out an email that lists the stakeholders who have provided status and who have not, taking advantage of peer pressure. They can also contact the superior of the stakeholder not providing status. The key is project managers asserting themselves in collecting information that they need to assess performance and to provide the necessary visibility to key stakeholders.

7.5 CASE STUDY

Phoenix Plane Parts Aerospace, Inc., known as P3A, is a major supplier of airplane components to the airline manufacturer Starlight Aerospace, Inc. (SA) in Denver, Colorado. P3A specializes in assembling components for different business jets produced by SA. It is becoming a leader in assembling airplane components made of composite material, provided by its Tier 1 suppliers. P3A has three sole suppliers for myriad composite parts and then assembles them into larger components for shipment to different aerospace manufacturers, the primary one being SA. P3A has approximately 7,000 employees and generates revenues close to $12 billion a year.

The growth of P3A has been phenomenal over the last two years, thanks in large part to its lucrative contract with SA to provide a fully assembled empennage for its series of business jet models. P3A has tried to maintain a small shop, craftsman perspective, but its success in this regard has made it very difficult to adapt to this growth. Its current processes to assemble components have been costly in terms of money, reputation, and its relationships with both suppliers and its primary customer, SA. Despite dramatic growth in revenues, the operating costs have skyrocketed so high that the profit margin has been declining each year. Labor problems have also increased, thanks in part to management seeking to reduce costs using layoffs and pursuing greater offshoring opportunities. Stockholders, especially institutional investors, are also upset and placing pressure to increase stock performance and dividend payouts.

Not surprisingly, P3A has many problems, the least of which include

- Excess inventory buffers and work-in-progress (WIP)
- Excessive scrap quantities and costs
- Excessive transportation time and costs
- Extended lead times
- High defect rates
- High warranty costs
- Incomplete or inaccurate specifications to suppliers
- Inefficient flow processes
- Lack of visibility of performance metrics
- Large batch runs
- Late deliveries from suppliers
- Late deliveries to SA
- Long setup times
- Lost or misplaced parts
- Lost or misplaced tools
- Low employee morale
- Machine equipment breakdown
- Nonstandard information systems

- Part shortages
- Pilferage of parts
- Poor quality
- Reliance on inspection
- Safety and health issues and costs
- Strained management–worker relations
- Undocumented processes and procedures

Based upon the long list of problems and the impact on the company and its longevity, the president and chief executive officer (CEO) and the other members of the board of directors (BoD) decided that something had to reverse this situation or the company could dissolve in five to ten years, closing the factory gates for good. The BoD agreed to establish a steering committee that would guide and oversee a program to implement Lean principles adopting the DMAIC cycle throughout the factory.

The steering committee comprised senior vice presidents and directors from each of the following functions and support services:

- Engineering and mechanics
- Facilities
- Human resources
- Information services
- Legal
- Material management
- Procurement
- Production planning and control
- Publications
- Quality assurance and control
- Representative union leadership for engineers and machinists
- Safety
- Sales and marketing
- Shop maintenance
- Supplier management
- Tooling
- Training and development

Several of the vice presidents and directors have multiple functional responsibilities, thereby limiting the number of stakeholders to a manageable level of 10 people. The vice president of engineering, David Letrino, was appointed to lead the steering committee. After several weeks of painstaking work, the steering committee developed a five-year plan to adopt Lean throughout the factory as a way to do business. Five major projects were identified to enable this transition to occur. Major start and stop milestone dates were identified for each project. The first project the committee selected was for the final assembly of the empennage for SA Model X38, a medium-range business jet popular throughout Latin and South America. The committee titled the project "Lean Empennage Advancement Project" (LEAP).

LEAP was to serve as a pilot to ascertain the challenges, issues, problems, and lessons learned that would lay the basis for managing the other four projects.

The steering committee selected Rob Jacobsen, senior project manager from engineering, to lead LEAP. Having previous experience leading Lean projects with other companies and being a certified Black Belt, he became the prime candidate for this pilot. His previous experience as an aerospace engineer in the empennage section of a factory with still another company also added to his becoming a prime choice.

Cindy McMartin, vice president of quality assurance and control, was selected as the project sponsor. She was to serve as the champion for LEAP, having experience in leading change management initiatives as they relate to manufacturing processes.

The empennage assembly team, or EAT as it is affectionately called, is responsible for assembling the major components of the tail of an aircraft to enable stability in flight. It includes the horizontal stabilizer, rudder, and vertical stabilizer. Each of the components is assembled separately in what are called subassemblies and then assembled together, called final assembly, as an integrated component by EAT. The empennage is then shipped to an SA manufacturing facility in Colorado.

The first order of business for Rob was to meet Cindy to become more knowledgeable about the work performed by the steering committee. During the meeting, he was presented with information needed to begin his own planning for LEAP:

- Five-year strategic plan for the Lean initiative
- Expectations and budget for the pilot project
- Business case
- Core team member assignments
- Program charter

The core team consisted of members from the first shift line responsible for assembling the empennage prior to shipment to SA. The core team consisted of a team lead, applicable manufacturing and industrial engineers, machinists, assemblers, composite specialists, quality control inspectors, drivers, and riveters. These people support LEAP on a part-time basis and are the considered equivalent to Green Belts. On an ad hoc basis, selected individuals serving as liaisons from finance, publications, information technology, sales and marketing, procurement, materials, and supplier management also participated on the project on an ad hoc basis or scheduled basis.

The company had two empennage assembly lines, consisting of two shifts. The assembly lines were located in the middle of the factory and the subassemblies for the empennage were then transported by vehicle to the final assembly area. Each line had its own set of equipment and supplies; these included but were not limited to cranes, lifts, stands, carts, tooling, toolkits, cargo loaders, tugs, functional and electrical test equipment, scaffolding, and seal and paint booths.

Despite efforts to control the flow of parts for the empennage through scheduling, the inventory buffers at selected points near the final assembly area were getting increasingly stacked with parts on a "just-in-case" basis because suppliers often delivered late to the subassembly areas and the parts sometime fell short of quality standards. The time requirements to deliver a completed empennage assembly did not allow for flexibility of rework. The standard practice was to inspect parts coming in from suppliers, conduct a quality inspection on relatively short notice, and, if the product failed, it was hoped the buffer had the necessary part. Unfortunately, on many occasions the quality of some parts, even in the buffer inventories, did not meet the standards because, during transport to the subassembly or to the final assembly area for the empennage, they were damaged.

Rob then elected to arrange for the first of many team meetings with his core team. The first order of business was to review the output of the steering committee and his discussions with Cindy. This information provided the context for LEAP as well as guidance for managing and leading the project in the future.

Working as a team, they developed a project charter that aligned with the one for the overall program. All core team members participated in updating the draft that he had presented to Cindy for feedback. She had some minor changes before the steering committee members were to review the charter. A draft of the charter was then circulated among steering committee members, all granting their approval. Then, Rob presented the charter one more time to the core team members for final feedback. No one on the team requested any changes. Cindy and Rob signed the charter, and she submitted it to the steering committee for final signatures.

Rob then convened the team to begin developing an overall strategy to manage the project. He explained that LEAP had some unknowns inasmuch as this was the first Lean project for the company. He suggested, and the team consented, that with the exception of the first stage of the DMAIC milestone dates were set for each stage; as each preceding stage got closer to completion, the succeeding one would then be planned in detail. Hence, the define stage was planned in detail within the flow time allowed by the start and stop milestones identified in the charter. As the define stage approached the completion milestone, the measure stage of DMAIC was planned in detail. This approach was adopted because LEAP was the first Lean project and the magnitude and complexity of the work effort was unknown. The approach gave the team some flexibility to adjust its plans accordingly. The concept applied is known as rolling wave, whereby as more information is known, the more in depth the planning can be for the next phase or stage.

In addition, the team elected to include gates at the end of each stage. This approach would preclude erroneously moving LEAP into the next stage with a serious oversight or need to perform rework.

The core team then met in subsequent sessions to perform the organizing and planning PM processes for the project. Rob realized from previous experience that detailed planning done unilaterally rarely worked. The people who had to perform the work would likely not follow the plans too seriously unless they had a sense of ownership and commitment and the best way to achieve both was to have them participate in the development of the deliverables for each PM process for LEAP. For example, the core team provided input on establishing the infrastructure (e.g., organization chart, procedures, etc.), work breakdown structure, time and cost estimates (where possible at this point in time), risk assessment, network diagram, schedule, and so on. The entire package, at a summary level, was presented to Cindy who, in turn, with Rob presented the output at the next steering committee meeting. The steering committee recommended some minor changes and then granted its approval contingent upon those changes being made. All changes were made.

Rob then worked with other functional managers on the floor, for example, electrical engineering, and the administrative functions, for example, finance, to procure their support for the project, specifically for acquiring part-time team members to perform relevant activities in the schedule.

Then, Rob determined that a kickoff meeting for LEAP, with Cindy attending, was necessary. After some minor input to the work done to date, the kickoff meeting was held. The meeting included all core and part-time members. The chairman of the committee, David Letrino, spoke briefly, followed by Cindy. Rob then presented a high-level overview on the project's background followed by a more extensive overview of the project infrastructure and plans. He also covered the next steps after giving everyone the opportunity to express comments, concerns, and insights. A scribe recorded all feedback during the session. If Rob, Cindy, or David could not answer a question or clarify something the request for feedback was recorded on an easel sheet titled a parking lot and one of the three promised (and did) get back to the pertinent person or persons requesting a response.

After the kickoff meeting, Rob, along with the core team, agreed to continue a two-day kaizen workshop that would compile and evaluate data and information related to the current process at the empennage assembly line.

Rob had a telephone conversation with the team leader of the empennage team who happened to note that no one from the customer or the suppliers was participating in LEAP. Rob was dumbfounded that such an oversight was not caught earlier by him or his core team, let alone the project sponsor or the steering committee. He knew that the team had to look at the entire supply chain for manufacturing, assembling, and delivering the empennage. He quickly made contact with some people responsible for interacting with both suppliers and the customer and was assured of their participation either through a P3A company liaison or representatives from suppliers and the customer. They, too, would attend the kaizen workshop and future ones and would be added to the project plans, where applicable.

Before the first kaizen workshop, Rob made every effort to ensure that rudimentary training on Lean was available, to include classroom and online training. The goal was not to make people experts on Lean or DMAIC but to have a common basic understanding and knowledge about the subject as well as being capable of communicating intelligently with each other, thereby reducing the opportunity for miscommunicating, poor coordination, and negative conflict.

He also conducted extensive preparations before the kaizen workshop. He collected relevant data and information as well as formulated a strategy for collecting the voice of the customer to acquire and clarify requirements that involved observations, interviews, documentation research, and data collection.

Cindy suggested that it would be a good idea to visit one of the suppliers' factories and the customer prior to the kaizen workshop. The purposes would be to become more familiar with their way of doing business and also to learn more about their needs and requirements. David agreed with her; and Rob, along with some other core team members, went to the suppliers' and customer's locations. He felt that this was a good way to start capturing the VOC in a document discussing their observations, insights, comments, and the like for use during and after the kaizen workshop.

The kaizen workshop lasted two days at an offsite location during a slow period in production. The project team covered many topics that were listed in the agenda prior to the meeting and sent along with a reminder for people to come prepared with the requisite data and information. At the session, the team started off with a review of the vision, goals, and objectives of the program and the LEAP project; they developed a high-level current value stream of the empennage assembly process; applied data and information to the value stream; reviewed the schedule for the define stage; presented observations, insights, and comments as well as entertained questions about the gemba at the suppliers' and customer's locations; presented results from the VOC efforts prior to the workshop; and conducted a lessons learned session for the workshop.

After the workshop, Rob and a select number of core team members prepared a presentation on the results of the define stage. This presentation was for the steering committee and was reviewed by the project sponsor and the chairman of the committee before presenting it to the steering committee. The reason for this approach was to identify and prepare for any shortcomings, problems, objections, or concerns that could cause some complication during the session. Two days prior to the steering committee meeting, Rob sent the final draft to the steering committee members. During the meeting, the committee members expressed their approval for the work done by LEAP. They also used the session to conduct a gate review and granted approval to proceed to the measure stage.

Prior to the session with the steering committee, Rob collected status against the schedule baseline. He collected this status and held weekly status review sessions with the core team and others who attended the meetings. Occasionally, he took corrective action to ensure that the current schedule and costs aligned with each prior to the next status review session. At the status meetings, he always started off reviewing the vision, goals, and objectives of the project as well as the risk assessment, critical issues, minutes from the previous meeting, and any concerns expressed by the stakeholders between meetings. At the end of each meeting, he would conduct a round robin to solicit feedback, thoughts, insights, comments, questions, and so on from attendees and also reviewed the upcoming weekly activities for the project, commonly referred to as the one-week look-ahead. He made a special effort to keep the meeting within its allotted timeframe and rarely, if ever, deviated from the agenda.

All material for the project, to include status review data and documentation, was stored on a server that allowed all team members to access data and information generated by the project. For stakeholders with restricted access, such as suppliers and contractors, nonproprietary files were stored on an intranet site using collaborative software.

Toward the end of the define stage, the core team began planning in detail for the measure stage. By the time the steering committee met to review the output of the define stage, the team had a game plan already built. A subsequent meeting was held after the team conducted a lessons learned for the define stage. The project sponsor and the chairman of the steering committee reviewed the plan for the measure stage and then both Cindy and Rob presented it to the steering committee, which granted its approval to proceed.

Rob then conducted a kickoff meeting for the measure stage for the project. Attendees at the session included core team members and other selected stakeholders. Although important, this kickoff meeting mainly covered the work for the measure stage.

The purpose of the measure stage is to amplify the collection of data and information about the current process that was compiled and received in the define stage. Special effort was made to drill down into the current process and collect or verify additional data and information. The team, for instance, identified and collected more data and information about the satisfiers and delighters of the customer, to use Kano jargon. It also expanded on the current value stream to ascertain areas performing well that satisfied the customer and those that provided potential opportunities for improvement. This information was then used to determine the critical inputs to the process as well as the requirements, also known as the critical-to-quality requirements.

Also important to the success of this stage was having all the team members understand the terminology used on the project. Although important for the define stage, it becomes even more so for this one and the succeeding stages. Rob collaborated, therefore, with core team members and others to develop a common glossary of terms. He also collaborated with the team to achieve consensus over a set of statistical tools and techniques to use for collecting, displaying, and eventually analyzing results (which occurs in the analyze stage).

During this stage, it became apparent that the milestone date for completion would have to slide two weeks. The complexity and effort to measure the performance of the current process was taking longer than expected. This situation meant the milestone date specified in the charter would have to change, which required formal approval. Rob first convened with the core team to explore options before formally submitting a request to Cindy for initial review and final approval by a change board that consisted of her and selected stakeholders, some of whom were on the steering committee. The options were clear: either reduce the scope or change the schedule. Rob and the team favored changing the schedule after performing an impact analysis based upon assessing the impact on cost, schedule, and quality. Cindy agreed and had Rob submit a formal request to the change board, which approved it after performing its own evaluation of the impact on future projects and the overall Lean initiative for the company.

Rob then made adjustments to the schedule after consulting with team members who performed activities affected by the changes. He also continued the same approach on managing and leading this stage as he did for the define one. He collected status data and information, held weekly review meetings, revisited the risk assessment, and ensured ongoing communication occurred among stakeholders according to the communications management plan.

Toward the end of this stage, he prepared, with input from the team, a report on the findings and any emergent recommendations for improvement as well as conducted a lessons learned session with relevant stakeholders.

One of the unique features that he performed on the project was encouraging the use of peer reviews among team members as they went about collecting and compiling data and generating information. These peer reviews helped to check the quality of work of individuals to ascertain if the right statistical measures, techniques, or charts were used and to ensure all standards in the project procedures were followed. Rob, with the consensus of the core team, saw this approach as a way to improve quality of the output throughout this stage and, therefore, minimize the amount of rework at the end of the stage. In other words, quality was built into the process, not waiting for inspection to determine if rework was necessary.

After passing the gate review for the measure stage, the team reviewed the data and information along with the current value stream map to determine the critical inputs to the process, identified the most important causes for the problems and issues in the define stage, and conducted additional data collection and analysis to substantiate existing findings.

Throughout the phase, Rob kept the team focused on the vision, goals, and objectives for the project, the critical-to-quality requirements, and had the team follow the schedule. He also ensured that all PM tools and techniques adopted in the define and measure stages were applied according to the consensus of the team. Again, as this stage came to a conclusion, the team planned out the next stage, conducted a lessons learned, and produced a report on the results. And, once again, the project team received approval from the steering committee to move forward to the next stage, improve.

The improve stage was the most exciting part of the DMAIC for the team. It required using the output of the measure and analyze stages and coming up with potential solutions to reduce waste in the empennage process. After several brainstorming sessions, the team came up with a list of recommendations that addressed 80% of the problems and issues that were high priorities as identified by the VOC. The team's recommendations were reflected in a future state value stream map along with expected standards of performance and accompanying metrics to detect significant variation when those recommendations were to be implemented. The recommendations were identified by priority using the prioritized list of problems, issues, and concerns from the VOC along with the associated corresponding benefits. Often these recommendations involved improvements that eliminated waste usually in one or more of these four areas: people, data, systems, and procedures.

Additionally, the team decided that first it would conduct a test of the future state on a much smaller scale before implementing the changes in the future value stream map. This pilot served as a way to determine the effectiveness of the recommendations shown in the future state value stream. The team decided to apply the recommendations to the vertical stabilizer subassembly process. This pilot was to help determine if the recommendations did improve performance and also to see if any unexpected problems might arise or if anything might be overlooked in the future value stream map.

The pilot proved to be a success. Some minor problems did occur but overall ended up as improvements, such as reducing inventories, improving setup times, speeding up cycle time, and decreasing the number of defective parts arriving at the assembly line. One of the significant recommendations embraced the concept of just-in-time delivery of some parts for the horizontal stabilizer. These parts mainly came from a supplier on the west coast of the United States. The supplier, having a representative on the team, had served as an effective stakeholder in communicating to his company the need to embrace JIT manufacturing and working closely with P3A. The production of these parts at the supplier's location was now in tandem with the takt time of the manufacturing line of P3A which, in turn, was getting in sync with P3A's customer, SA. The team also conducted a risk assessment to anticipate any of the problems that could arise during the pilot and, if they did occur, and some did, apply the appropriate response to ascertain its effectiveness. The risk assessment approach used was failure modes and effects analysis (FMEA).

The pilot proved successful with some minor glitches. Substantial improvements were realized in the subassembly process of the horizontal stabilizer. Rob conducted a lessons learned with the team and other stakeholders in the process. He also got with the team and prepared a detailed plan to manage and lead the control stage, the last one in the DMAIC cycle. He also produced a report on the results of the pilot that was presented to the project sponsor and the steering committee. After a review of the cost, schedule, and quality performance for the improve stage and the report, the steering committee granted its approval to proceed to the next and final stage, control.

The purpose of the control stage is to implement the improved process on a much grander scale, in this case the empennage assembly. Because two assembly lines existed, Rob with the consent of the project sponsor and the steering committee decided to implement the improved process on one of the assembly lines before doing so with the other. This strategy offered several advantages. It would minimize the complexity of transitioning the two large assembly lines at the same time. It would allow time to work out the bugs in the revised process and take whatever corrective action necessary. It would enable P3A to deliver to SA an empennage and not involve a total shutdown of the delivery of the product to the customer if a showstopper occurred. It would provide for a smoother transition for the other empennage assembly line based upon the lessons learned from the first assembly line.

The plans for the control stage had three major deliverables. The first one was the preparation deliverable. This deliverable entailed developing all the procedures and training needed to ensure a smooth transition from the current process to the new one as described in the future value stream map. Another deliverable was the measures and metrics to monitor the effectiveness of the future process and to ascertain if, and when, corrective action was necessary. The third deliverable was to verify whether the vision, goals, and objectives, as well as the expectations and requirements of the customer, had been met either through an audit or a postimplementation review, or both.

A final report was delivered to the steering committee, which reviewed the vision, goals, and objectives of the project. The report also presented a balanced view of the successes and failures during the project, most of which were extracted from the lessons learned compiled at the end of each stage. A review of the overall cost, schedule, and quality performance was also conducted and recorded in the report. The customer, SA, sent a letter to the president and CEO of P3A congratulating the team for reducing the reject rate and improving the cycle time, making a big difference on SA's own reject rate and cycle time delivering airplanes to its customers, not to mention a substantial decline in late delivery penalties.

Rob closed all open contracts before officially closing the project. He also compiled and archived the information for the project. Finally, he planned for individual and team awards for stakeholders on the project.

7.6 PROJECT MANAGEMENT WORKS WITH DMAIC, TOO

As with using the PDCA cycle, PM plays an instrumental role in the success of a Lean project applying DMAIC. Imagine the complexity of managing a project like LEAP without any PM. The probability of failure would be greater than that of success. With a PM, however, the probability of success exceeds that of failure if for no other reason in that it provides velocity, that is, speed and direction toward a vision. Just the complexity alone compels a large or even a small organization to use PM. As with using the PDCA cycle, the degree or extent of PM applied depends on the scale and complexity of a project. The project manager, along with the feedback of key stakeholders, makes that determination. The LEAP example demonstrates the power of buy-in when determining how much PM is enough on projects so that stakeholders have a sense of ownership and commitment in their project. In other words, PM for a Lean project is more than numbers, schedules, and methods. It is more about people working together for a common outcome.

7.7 GETTING STARTED CHECKLIST

Question	Yes	No
1. For your Lean project using the DMAIC cycle, do you face any of these challenges (and have a way to address them): Obtaining data and information? Narrowing down what is critical? Overcoming resistance to change? Defining the problem or issue? Abandoning biases and unfounded assumptions? Finding qualified and knowledgeable people? Giving people sufficient time to support the project? Transferring to operations? Inculcating accountability? Resolving differences? Following the stages? Lacking knowledge and understanding about DMAIC? Selecting the right candidate projects? Focusing on the long-term? Creating a sense of urgency? Achieving simplicity? Defining terminology? Obtaining customer feedback? Ensuring reliability of performance?		
2. When defining your project, do you consider the following: Organization mission statement? Steering committee membership? Project charter? Project sponsor? Statement of work?		
3. When organizing your project, do you consider the following: Communication management plan? Data repository structure and content? Organization chart? Procedures and workflows? Roles, accountabilities, and authorities (RAAs)?		

Question	Yes	No
Software tools? Team meeting and their management? Self-assessment on level of knowledge about Lean? Reporting requirements?		
4. When planning your project, do you consider the following: Work breakdown structure? Detail and rollup schedules? One or multiple releases of the product or service? Risk assessment? Resource utilization? Time and cost estimating? Critical issues?		
5. When executing your project, do you consider the following: Kickoff meeting? Performance baselines? Change management?		
6. When monitoring and closing your project, do you consider the following: Detail and summary performance metrics? Frequency of reporting? Change management?		
7. When closing your project, do you consider the following: Lessons learned? Contract closure? Requirements verification? Customer validation? Data compilation and archiving? Team celebration?		

8

Ten Final Thoughts about Lean

Lean has been around for a few years now. However, common perceptions and misperceptions, some accurate and some less so, exist that necessitate some discussion as to their veracity.

8.1 WHAT LEAN IS NOT

To a large extent, Lean has become the poster child for the postindustrial world. Indeed, it has contributed immensely to the profitability and efficient functioning of many public and private institutions because of its emphasis on satisfying the customer. However, some perceptions and misperceptions exist that can jeopardize the value of Lean, maybe not in the short run, but in the long run, and can have devastating consequences for an organization. Most of these perceptions and misperceptions center on what Lean is not.

Lean is not an excuse to circumvent controls. When Lean emphasizes the need to please the customer, it does not mean a company must loosen or eliminate critical controls, for example, financial or operational, thereby putting a public or private institution at risk with, for example, the government, public, or investors. In many circumstances, controls are necessary and they may, at times, stay in place even if it means creating some waste and, yes, displeasing the customer. In this regard, the customer isn't always right. Too often, Lean focuses so much on customer satisfaction that it jeopardizes the long-term survivability of the customer or the company. Although a rarity, it has happened. In some cases, approvals are necessary before a process is considered complete. The desire for speed and direction may be what the customer considers more important; for example, the plane breaks up in flight because appropriate controls were eliminated that served a valid purpose in the manufacturing process. Surely under such circumstances, customer satisfaction is sacrificed in the long run. Some waste is necessary under certain circumstances even if it means not pleasing the customer. That is why it is very important for Lean project managers to know the priorities according to what the customer wants and determine whether they are feasible. Project managers should ensure that a charter exists as well as develop a meaningful SOW and requirements matrix, and conduct risk assessments and gate reviews to ensure that controls are not eliminated or weakened, and, if so, make sure an audit trail exists related to decisions made and actions taken.

Lean is not a one-time affair. Many times Lean, as do many other initiatives in companies, becomes the flavor of the month. The topic circumvents just about everything else that is important and, indeed, many events become interpreted, rightly or wrongly, from a Lean perspective. Like a little boy with a hammer, everything becomes a nail. "Leanese" is spoken even when people sometimes do not even know what they are saying. Then, suddenly, the enthusiasm runs out because no more nails exist and interest in Lean declines. In some cases, it dies a slow death. A danger exists for a Lean project in the nature of the project itself. It, like all projects, ends once the goals and objectives have been achieved and the customer is pleased. Oftentimes, after the kudos and celebrations are over, followthrough no longer continues and the results of the Lean project die a slow death and, yes, the customer regresses back to the old way of doing business. Lean projects need followup on their results to avoid this scenario. Otherwise, in time the gains yield to the losses. Good project managers of Lean projects recognize this tendency and, while managing the project, consider what is needed to sustain the results achieved. In other words, they also plan for the future after the Lean project completes. They may not develop a full comprehensive plan but they communicate the need to consider what happens after a project fulfills its goals and objectives. Project managers should raise this concern during requirements analysis and building the WBS.

Lean has value even if it does not result in change. This one is partially true in that it increases people's awareness and knowledge about an existing process and also provides opportunities for greater communication and coordination. However, stopping at that point is wasteful. Many Lean projects have consumed innumerable people, considerable time, and other resources to come up with recommendations to improve processes that will satisfy customers. This can be very gratifying to a team and a customer. However, and it happens more often than not, the recommendations seem to fall by the wayside if a Lean project concludes at that point. Not implementing recommendations is not only a waste of organizational resources and simply adding to the overhead, it can be very demoralizing to a team that came up with the recommendations but nothing further occurred. It is not too difficult to understand why this circumstance frequently exists, and it goes deeper than believing that people resist change. Reasons include a fear of the consequences of making a change, such as job loss or decrease in managerial or executive power, union resistance, ego protection, politics, and many others. The point is that people, from shareholders to employees, have invested blood, sweat, toil, and tears, as Churchill would say, to improve a process that will satisfy a customer. If this tends to be a trend in an organization, project managers will face considerable morale issues as negativism and game-playing become a higher priority than achieving the vision for the project. Not seeing the fruits of their labor being implemented can prove depressing and, ultimately, demoralizing. Toward the end of their projects, project managers need to emphasize the necessity of pushing for sustainable change, which means addressing the implementation of recommendations. Indeed, they should incorporate in their plans sustaining and operational considerations, planning activities for the next phase. In many cases, Lean projects have responsibility for implementing their recommendations but that is not always the case. In large companies, however, coming up with recommendations may be separate from implementing them.

Lean is the same as re-engineering. This is partially true. Many of the tools and techniques of Lean can be used on re-engineering projects and vice versa. That is, however, about all the similarity that exists. The focus on Lean is the customer; in re-engineering it is on efficiency. Re-engineering projects seek to obliterate an existing process and totally rebuild a new one, often without the participation of the people doing the work. The results are often wholesale slaughter of processes, not to mention jobs and careers. For the most part, Lean emphasizes a more measured approach toward change. The emphasis is on continuous improvement in the pursuit of perfection. It builds upon the past, eliminating in a process anything that does not add value to the customer. Lean emphasizes engagement and relies on the people who do the work to identify improvements and, it is hoped, their implementation. It reduces the fear factor substantially because they have a say about a process. Project managers of Lean projects must stress and encourage stakeholder engagement to avoid the disastrous consequences of re-engineering that had occurred in the past. That is the true value of a plan to manage and lead stakeholders. By ascertaining their degree of interest and power concerning a Lean project by using stakeholder analysis, a project manager can take action accordingly to ensure greater contributions from stakeholders.

Lean is relevant only in manufacturing environments. Lean may have received visibility for success in the manufacturing environment, but, as this book shows, it can be applied in just about any environment, including the office environment. Many office environments still adhere to the old business model by Frederick Taylor, treating everything as if it were a manufacturing line. Or, they may apply Lean in a small way, which is fine but does not capitalize on its power. Many medical environments are prime examples where Lean could prove valuable. The administrative way of doing business in many medical facilities is replete with examples of processes needing Lean. The medical laws, such as HIPAA, can only be blamed so much. In many offices, and not just medical facilities, applying 5S is about the only extent to which Lean is applied, and usually only one or two of the Ss are used: sort and shine. Lean is so much more than 5S and the office environment, more out of rigid adherence to the status quo, often fails to leverage Lean as a way to reduce overhead and become more responsive to customers. Project managers of Lean projects in nonmanufacturing environments should apply the same rigor in applying Lean concepts, tools, and techniques that occurs in manufacturing industries. These concepts, tools, and techniques can be identified in the WBS, schedule, and responsibility assignment matrices.

Lean is a way to reduce headcount. This perception is the gorilla in the room. Yet, that is precisely how many people at the executive levels view Lean. So many times public and private people talk Lean through both sides of their mouths as a popular saying goes. They will often say, "People are our greatest resource," but, at the same time or just afterward, lay people off while embracing and applying Lean. Lean is an excellent way to reduce overhead but the emphasis is on providing value to the customer. Unfortunately, the leadership of an organization fails often intentionally or inadvertently in communicating that Lean is another convenient way for thinning out the ranks. Naturally, after one or two successful Lean projects and layoffs soon follow, people become skeptical and, rightly or wrongly, perceive Lean simply as a means to chop heads. When this situation occurs Lean's value shifts from something being embraced to being avoided, sabotaged. Project managers of Lean projects need to be aware of this perception that can arise because it can be a worry for some team members. If team members perceive Lean as contributing to even the potential loss of their jobs their engagement in the project is likely to wane and could result in subtle or overt resistance. Project managers need to have the support of an organization's leadership to embrace Lean projects by assuring people that they will not lose their jobs due to Lean projects and to demonstrate assurance by rewarding, not punishing, people for doing a great job applying Lean. However, the tone starts at the top and if senior and executive management communicate the wrong message even the best of project managers will face a difficult battle to complete a Lean project.

8.2 WHAT LEAN IS

Lean is a way to engage people. Getting people involved in removing waste is essential to increase ownership and reduce resistance to change. People who know part or all of a process will likely have a good idea how best to improve it by eliminating waste and satisfying a customer. They will also feel less threatened than if a group of process engineers simply goes and streamlines a process without any consultation. However, if team members feel they are merely pawns, even if encouraged to participate, they do so perfunctorily. Fear of job loss is a real issue on a Lean project. Just think about it. If a company removes waste and operates more efficiently and effectively with less, why would people want to participate in something that means the destruction of their livelihood? Yet, executive management often ignores this common sense realization by making statements that ignore negative consequences and stress enhancing shareholder value and profitability. Streamlining a critical process and laying off people, at least in the short run, will shoot profits up; frequently, in the long run it will shoot profits down. It behooves project managers, therefore, to get people engaged throughout the life cycle of their Lean project. Many of the tools of PM encourage greater engagement, such as having the people who do the work help build the plans as well as execute them. People on a Lean project should be rewarded, too, to demonstrate that senior management values them as well as their contributions. One way to do that is to assign them to other projects rather than letting them go after the Lean project they supported. Nothing can kill morale faster than laying people off once a Lean project has demonstrated uncontestable value to an organization. Unfortunately, sometimes the business models in some companies result in forcing immediate realization of savings and the easiest way to do that is to cut heads. When that happens, the ripple effects radiate through the ranks elsewhere in an organization and the motto "Lean is mean" becomes the phrase of the day. Engaging people is one way to offset this negative perception; the other way is to reward for performance.

Lean is more than the bottom line. This perception is tied to the previous one. However, it goes one step further. It involves satisfying the customer. That's right; the focus is on the customer, not simply gutting an organization to reduce costs. The financial bottom line is just one aspect of Lean to consider. It does no good for a company to do everything it can to reduce costs in the short run but in the long run jeopardizes its very existence. Short-term gain can lead to long-term pain. Customers still need reliable, sustainable support beyond a project. Nothing can kill Lean faster than, ironically, a long degradation of services or products delivered to a customer because Lean projects emphasized cost reduction over everything else. The "bean counters" may be happy but the rest of the organization can suffer. True, efficiency is important, but so is effectiveness. Without both, the zeal for Lean can quickly lose favor among the rank and file. Project managers of Lean projects need to emphasize and take a balanced view of Lean on their projects. They need to consider all options and consequences and subscribe to a strategic view of their projects. They not only must think about the immediate requirements of their project, such as cost, schedule, and quality but also the longer-term ones. A good systems perspective, a risk assessment, and requirements prioritization are three solid ways to ensure that Lean projects are more than trimming the bottom line. In some circumstances, as noted earlier in the book, some waste may be necessary and would be of no value in eliminating it, such as legal compliance.

Lean requires an investment in time, money, and effort. As most people know today, quality is not free. For many years that was not necessarily the perception. Times have changed, of course, and quality, of which Lean is a subset and some people would say the other way around, has costs associated with it. These costs are really investments to ensure that a quality product or service is delivered to a customer. However, as with all investments, a breakeven point exists where the gains start to decline. As an investment, Lean projects require a considerable application of time, money, and effort to achieve success. Time, money, and other resources, especially labor, are needed to train people. Time, money, and other resources are needed to enhance understanding of what exactly the customer wants and improving a process accordingly. This common sense, of course, is anything but common. What often happens is that the pressure is so intense many Lean projects are done on the cheap: little time, money, and effort are invested. For many reasons, many senior managers and executives see Lean as important and, despite the huge potential returns, financial or otherwise, scrimp on the investment. Not surprisingly, many Lean projects end up working with shoestring budgets and the recommendations and actual improvements are less than stellar. Confidence in Lean in general and in these projects in particular wanes. In time, Lean no longer becomes the flavor of the month and recommendations for improvement are no longer considered seriously. Project managers of Lean projects need to exercise assertiveness in this regard. They must perform realistic planning. When confronted with a series of directions that will only lead a Lean project to disaster, they must provide alternatives and, in some cases, state that a project is not doable under the current conditions. This is not as easy as one would think when project managers have senior executives hovering over them and they have a weak project sponsor. Many Lean projects are so lean, ironically, their fate is predictable and, yet, many project managers sit idle in the face of such circumstances. They often settle for projects that are akin to having a champagne taste but having only a dime to spend.

Lean is a never-ending journey. Even though a project is by nature short lived, the reality is a Lean one is not. Lean requires continuous application of its concepts, tools, and techniques to improve processes as an organization seeks to satisfy the customer. Both circumstances and the needs of the customer are going to change over time. Nothing in a work environment is static. People leave, profits decline, demand goes unexpectedly up, and new tools and techniques come into existence and upset existing ways of doing business. These situations require continually keeping tabs on processes. With change often comes the need for improvement. Just because a Lean project ends, it does not mean additional future improvements for a process are unnecessary. It is important, therefore, that project managers of Lean projects never lose sight of this fact. They need to plan not for the end of their projects but also for future Lean ones that may capitalize on the output of the former. Taken from a different angle, project managers of Lean projects need to recognize that implications of their projects continue long after completing the current ones. They need to instill that thought into the minds of the stakeholders and plan for the potential repeatability of their projects. A good project closing is important at the end of each phase, whether using the PDCA or DMAIC life cycles. Performing archiving and conducting lessons learned sessions are just two of the many ways to prepare for potential future projects that may address the same process.

Lean combined with project management is an exercise in Lean. For many people, PM is the antithesis of Lean. They see PM as layers of bureaucracy and control that quite simply adds to the overhead of an organization. They view PM as merely a roadblock preventing people from getting the real work done. Hence, the popularity of the term PM lite and no one really knows exactly what that means other than less PM. PM lite is often viewed by some as an excuse to apply what is euphemistically referred to as "seat of your pants" PM. Although a minimal degree of PM may be warranted for certain projects the lack of any PM as defined in this book is a surefire prescription for disaster. It is true that Lean requires speed and flexibility to develop and implement recommendations to improve processes that please the customer, but it is also true that no PM, and no project leadership, can also result in slowing a project and hamstringing adaptability. The best perspective is to view PM as a backbone to manage and lead a Lean project. Not all backbones are the same for each person because people vary in height, weight, and so on. A six-foot backbone will not serve a five-foot person very well and vice versa. The backbone needs to be appropriate for the size and shape of the body. The same concept applies to PM on Lean projects. The breadth and depth of project management concepts, tools, and techniques being applied must be conducive to the context in which a Lean project finds itself. Project managers of Lean projects must demonstrate this wisdom about PM to show PM is an exercise in Lean. They can communicate and work closely with key stakeholders, for example, to determine the degree of PM to apply and talk to other project managers who are, or were, responsible for other Lean projects of a similar nature. They can also establish metrics to determine how well their processes are furthering or hindering project performance, such as progressing through its life cycle.

8.3 PROJECT MANAGEMENT AND LEAN: ONE FINAL THOUGHT

Lean continues to pick up momentum across many industries. When an organization decides to do a Lean project, it usually means that the business case demonstrates an improvement in many areas, financial or otherwise. In the end, a Lean project should demonstrate improvements in efficiency and effectiveness. PM is the most efficient and effective way to achieve such results. Otherwise, a Lean project will go down an endless trail, never ending, like the wheels on a bus going round and round.

Glossary

A3: A single page containing critical information about an issue, problem, or concern; specific elements may include a description, tentative date for completion, responsibility for completion, and any additional pertinent information.

Affinity diagram: The grouping of disparate items or elements into categories based upon some common criterion or criteria.

Andon: A visual status device, or some other medium, that indicates the status of a process and when a problem arises during its execution.

Assumptions: Suppositions or perceptions assumed to be facts until proven otherwise.

Autonomation: A machine, often using an intelligent agent, which enables it to detect a production problem, causes the process to cease, and alerts the need for assistance to resolve.

Backlog: Accumulating a workload with content that remains open, has not been prioritized, and scheduled for being addressed, for example, deployment of a fix.

Baseline: (1) A target used to compare current performance with a stakeholder (e.g., customer, expectations); (2) an agreement between two or more stakeholders on what constitutes something, such as a product or service description, schedule, or budget.

Batch-and-queue: Accumulating parts, products, and the like in large lots that will subsequently be placed in a queue for use in a future process.

Benchmarking: Comparing a company's process performance with that of similar vein considered "best-in-class" and then improving its performance accordingly.

Best practice: A method or practice considered by peers (e.g., experts, organizations, etc.) as superior to other methods or practices and adopted within a given environment.

Brownfield: An existing facility and organization employing mass production processes, methods, and techniques.

Burndown: Accounting for completion rate of deliverables (e.g., products) over a given time period.

Burnup: Accounting for deliverables completed (e.g., products) over a given time period.

Business value: Also known as value-added; it is based upon what the customer deems worthwhile and for which it is willing to pay.

Cause-and-effect diagram: A tool that displays the relationship (e.g., casual or correlative) among two or more variables.

Cell: Also known as chaku-chaku; a method for arranging machinery in a U-shaped and counterclockwise manner, to take a part from one machine to the next, followed by another part.

Chaku-chaku: See cell.

Change management: (1) Policies, processes, and procedures to detect, analyze, evaluate, and implement changes to all baselines; (2) a disciplined approach toward recording, evaluating, and tracking changes.

Changeover: A machine transferring from a current operation to a new different one.

Check sheet: A log or form to record, compile, and analyze counts of data, items, and events, among others, for subsequent use in statistical calculations.

Closing: Concluding a project efficiently and effectively by ensuring all criteria have been met, archiving documents, and so on.

Consensus: Stakeholders understand, accept, and support a decision or action despite reservations.

Constraint: Any restriction that limits potentially higher performance of a process or operation.

Contingency plan: One or more alternative defined responses to issues, problems, risks, and the like that arise.

Continuous flow: Also simply referred to as flow, the ongoing uninterrupted execution of an element, for example, people or parts, within a process; often described as a process's ideal state whereby no stoppages or scrap exists.

Continuous process improvement: Also known as process improvement, a perspective taken that through analysis of a process or operation, ongoing improvement can occur with the expressed purpose of satisfying the customer.

Control chart: A visual display of information showing patterns of behavior over a period of time.

Cost estimating: Determining how much a project, deliverable, tasks, and so on will cost based upon a set of assumptions, data, and calculations.

Cost-benefit analysis: Determining if the cost of improvement activities achieves sufficient benefit to warrant proceeding with a change.

Critical-to-quality characteristics: Activities or deliverables that the customer deems important to achieve satisfaction.

Current-state value stream map: A visual display of the sequence and interaction of elements of a process as they currently exist.

Customer: (1) The person or organization that receives the output (e.g., product or service) from a process; (2) a person or organization for which the project exists.

Customer satisfaction: The outcome of a process that provides a product or service meeting a recipient's requirements.

Customer specification: A requirement identified by a recipient of a product or service.

Daily stand-up: A brief session that team members attend to discuss what happened since the previous session, what to do in the interim to the next session, and any impediments a team member faces.

Dashboard: A visual display providing reports on progress, trends, and other concerns, such as potential risks.

Data: Raw facts that have no meaning until converted into information.

Data flow diagram: A graphic displaying the movement of raw facts through one or more processes that generate output, such as raw facts or information, either to another process or an entity or both.

Data stratification: Dividing data into smaller populations to facilitate analysis and reporting.

Defect: A flaw in the output of a process, potentially resulting in not meeting customer expectations.

Defect rate: The number of rejected items in a product or service failing to meet customer expectations related to requirements or specifications.

Defining: Determining in advance what the project will achieve.

Deliverable: An artifact that may be included in the delivery of the final product or service to the customer.

Design of experiment: A technique used to show the relationship of two or more variables and the expected results of their interaction.

Design of Six Sigma: Abbreviated DFSS, the goal of this approach is to develop and design a new process using Six Sigma tools and techniques.

DMAIC: An acronym of a common Six Sigma approach to improve an existing process; *d*efine, *m*easure, *a*nalyze, *i*mprove, and *c*ontrol.

Earned value management: A schedule and cost performance management technique comparing and monitoring planned and actual outcomes.

Executing: Implementing the plan for a project to achieve goals and objectives.

Facilitator: A neutral individual who helps team members to collaborate in an environment that enables open communications and trusting relationships.

Failure mode and effect analysis: A tool to determine what could potentially go awry with a process or product and the reason or reasons for its failure.

Five S (5S): Removing waste from a process within an organization; it involves five activities: sort, straighten, scrub, systematize, and standardize.

Five Whys: A method to ascertain the root cause of a problem or issue by repeatedly, often five times but sometimes more, asking "Why?" and then developing and implementing a lasting solution.

Flow: Refer to continuous flow.

Frequency plot: A visual tool to display how often an event occurs.

Future-state value stream: A graphical flow depicting a process in an anticipated improved state which serves as a "stepping stone" leading to an ideal state in which perfect continuous flow occurs.

Gemba: Visiting the location of where the work is performed with the intent to understand the work and how to add or improve value for the customer.

Genchi Genbutsu: Refer to Gemba; translated from Japanese to mean "go and see."

Greenfield: A new facility and organization employing best practices to processes, methods, and techniques.

Heijunka: Known as schedule leveling, a technique to produce parts, products, and the like that reduces variation in production, resulting in a smooth process flow.

Heijunka box: A tool to control production via Kanban at fixed time intervals.

Histogram: A series of bars, each reflecting the frequency of occurrence of a variable within a specific class or category.

Hoshin Kanri: A systematic approach for decision-making at the strategic and tactical levels of an organization to achieve business objectives via projects aligning with those objectives.

Ideal-state value stream map: A graphical flow depicting a process in a perfect state providing only value-added operations.

Impediment: A business or technical issue, problem, or other concern negatively affecting and restricting the continuous flow of a process.

Information: Data that have no value to a person or organization.

Information radiator: An informational display providing self-explanatory content about a project or a process.

Interrelationship digraph: A diagram showing the causal relationship and interaction among different variables, elements, processes, and so on.

Inventory: Parts, products, data, and other work items that remain incomplete.

Jidoka: See autonomation.

Just-in-time: A system that provides the right amount of resources (e.g., part) at the right time, at the right place, thereby reducing inventories, and so on and allowing for continuous flow.

Kaikaku: A radical version of Lean, such as what is referred to as breakthrough kaizen.

Kaizen: Continuous incremental improvement in a process or product in a way that increases effectiveness and reduces waste.

Kanban: A signal that manages or regulates the flow of resources through the value stream by notifying upstream, for example, production or activities.

Lead time: The cumulative time a customer must wait to receive the final product after submitting an order or request.

Leading: Motivating people to achieve the desired results of a project.

Lean: (1) A customer-focused approach that concentrates on providing value by eliminating waste and increasing quality; (2) a manufacturing philosophy consisting of concepts, principles, tools, and practices to improve supply chain performance based on meeting the requirements of the customer.

Lean Six Sigma: The combination of Lean and Six Sigma techniques adopted by Motorola to reduce waste.

Lessons learned: A document containing a postevaluation of a project.

Level selling: Profiling a process to reduce surges in demand while at the same time satisfying its requirements.

Management: Stakeholders who participate in setting the strategic direction of a company.

Matrix: A table displaying the relationship between two or more variables or elements, such as condition and response.

Measurement plan: A document describing the approach to measure how to employ a tool or technique to analyze process performance.

Milk run: Using a transport medium, such as a van or truck, for multiple pickups at several locations.

Modeling: Constructing diagrams reflecting processes, procedures, and components of a system, and so on as a way to improve understanding and develop ideas.

Monitoring and controlling: Assessing how well a project uses plans and its organization to meet the project's vision, goals, and objectives.

Monument: Technology or site, due to its unique requirements or characteristics, requiring resources or information to wait in a queue until needed for processing.

Muda: Any activity or item in a value stream that does not add value.

Multimachine working: Used to build cells by training workers to operate different types of equipment, usually through cross-training.

Mura: Unevenness or variation in flow, resulting in waste.

Muri: Stress on a system, such as people and equipment, resulting in waste.

Needs: Requirements that must be minimally met by a project.

Non-value-added: (1) Processes, operations, activities, or products that do not add value to the customer; (2) tasks and output that do not contribute toward achieving the vision of a project.

One-touch setup: Any changeover requiring a very short time to occur.

Open book management: All managerial information, such as financial, related to a process, operation, or activity, being accessible by all employees having an interest when providing value to a customer.

Operation: One or more activities that workers perform to execute a process.

Organizing: Employing resources efficiently and effectively to manage a project.

Outsourcing: Having vendors, buyers, and the like be responsible to produce part or all of the deliverables for a company.

Pareto chart: Graphically displaying the frequency of occurrence of an event or categories of events vis-à-vis other events or categories.

Pattern: Processes and practices, often referred to as best practices, identified to solve recurring problems.

Perfection: Seeking to eliminate waste to enable continuous flow in the value stream according to takt time.

Plan, do, check, act: (1) Abbreviated as PDCA, an iterative cycle to address problems, issues, and other circumstances to improve performance that results in better quality; (2) it consists of four phases: plan (objective), do (implement), check (verify), and act (revise).

Planning: Determining the activities to execute the vision of the project, assigning who will perform them, and identifying when they must start and stop.

Poka-yoke: Using a procedure or device to prevent an error or defect from moving forward in the value stream and being delivered to a customer.

Process: One or more operations to provide a product or service, for example, to a customer.

Process owner: The person responsible for executing and providing output for a process.

Process villages: A grouping of activities and machines to perform an operation within a process.

Processing time: The time that a product or service requested by a customer is being designed and built to requirements.

Product backlog: The incomplete, or remaining, work that piles up over time.

Product family: An interchangeable group of related products or services enabling the mix and match of elements during production.

Product vision: A brief description, usually one or two sentences, of a project deliverable using business terminology.

Project: A discrete set of activities performed logically to attain a specific result, for example, deliver a service or product.

Project champion: A person, usually at the executive level, setting and sustaining the direction and momentum throughout a project's life cycle.

Project charter: A document defining the business and technical parameters of a project.

Project management: The tools, knowledge, and techniques to lead, initiate, plan, organize, execute, monitor and control, and close a project.

Project manager: The person having overall accountability to complete a project.

Project team: The people brought together to produce one or more deliverables.

Prototype: A model of the final deliverable or service to enable stakeholders to adjust accordingly to satisfy requirements.

Pugh matrix: A technique to determine the best solution to a problem or issue.

Pull: Moving information, resources, and so on from the end of the value stream (e.g., delivery to the customer) to the beginning of the value stream (e.g., request or order) upon receiving a signal to deliver a product or service.

Push: Moving information, instructions, resources, and so on from the beginning of the value stream (e.g., design) to the end of the value stream (e.g., delivery) based upon forecasting a customer's need for a product or service.

Quality function deployment (QFD): Decision-making involving a multidisciplinary team focusing on customer needs and expectations early on in the value stream as well as providing measurable consistent performance.

Queue time: The time a resource, part, or product waits to proceed forward in the value stream.

Requirements documentation: The criteria to deliver the final product or service to a customer.

Responsibility assignment matrix: A chart showing the assignments and level of responsibility of people assigned to tasks identified in a work breakdown structure (WBS).

Root cause: The real factor contributing to a defect; by addressing the root cause the defect disappears.

Scatter plot: Also known as a scattergram, a tool showing the relationship, causal or correlative, between two factors.

Schedule: A road map displaying the sequence and times to accomplish the vision of a project.

Scope: (1) The result of a project within the specifications or requirements; (2) anything not within the specifications or requirements is excluded from being produced.

Scope creep: A gradual uncontrollable expansion of features and functions of the product or service delivered to the customer.

Scope management: A disciplined approach to identify and focus on the vision for a project.

Seiketsu: Refer to 5S; translated as systematize, or maintain.

Seiri: Refer to 5S; translated as sort, or separation.

Seiso: Refer to 5S; translated as scrub, or clean up.

Seiton: Refer to 5S; translated as straighten, or arrange and identify.

Senior management: Superiors of a project manager.

Sensei: A master teacher, especially in the context of Lean, having mastery of relevant tools and techniques.

Seven forms of waste: (1) Identified by Taiichi Ohno: transportation, waiting, overproduction, defects, inventory, motion, excess processing; (2) recently, two more have been added to the list, unmotivated workforce and safety.

Shitsuke: Refer to 5S; translated as standardize, or consistent.

Single minute exchange of dies: Tools and techniques employed to reduce changeover times, also referred to as SMED.

SIPOC: A flowchart that describes the relationship of five elements within, for example, a value stream (suppliers, inputs, process, outputs, and customers).

Situation target proposal: Also referred to as STP, a report explaining the current circumstances, the desired end state, and the means to achieve the vision.

Six Sigma: A method applied among disciplines and organizations alike emphasizing quantitative measures to reduce variation in a flow; an example would be using a statistical process control chart.

Spaghetti chart: A diagram displaying the route a product proceeds along through a value stream, often revealing its circuitous travel from one operation or location to another.

Span of control: The number of individuals that a leader can effectively control to accomplish goals and objectives of a project.

Sponsor: A senior manager with single authority to ensure a project is properly supported.

Stakeholder: A person or organization having an interest in the outcome of a project.

Stakeholder analysis: Identifying and analyzing the individuals or organizations participating in current and future value streams.

Standard work: A description of an operation or activity consisting of information such as execution time, takt time task sequence, and parts inventory to complete an activity.

Statement of work: A detailed description of the functions and features of a final product and service for delivery to a customer.

Statistical process control: A method for tracking and monitoring performance of a process, paying particular attention to variation.

Subject matter expert: An individual who is an authoritative source for guidance, information, and problem resolution.

Supplier: An internal or external entity providing one or more inputs to a process that results in delivery of a product or service to a customer.

Takt time: (1) A German word meaning "beat"; (2) the production time divided by the rate of customer demand, or consumption; (3) ideally, production pace is aligned with customer demand.

Three (3) Gen: Three gen is a technique involving going to a customer's site; observing activity; and obtaining reliable data to improve process performance.

Three (3) P: Three P is production, preparation, process, whereby a multidisciplinary team gathers together during the design phase of a value stream and identifies opportunities to remove waste.

Throughput time: The combination of processing and queue time for a product or service to be delivered to a customer.

Tollgates: Also referred to as check point reviews or simply gates, specific meetings with stakeholders at certain stages of a project to determine whether to proceed from one stage to another or make a change in direction.

Total productive maintenance: Also referred to as TPM, methods applied to machinery to ensure its ability and capacity to perform its purpose and ensure continuous flow.

Tree diagrams: A graphic to display the relationships among variables.

Turn-back analysis: Reviewing the flow of a value stream to determine at what point scrap or rework occurs.

Unit cost: The total money to produce, store, market, and sell a specific component of a product or service.

Validation: Determining a product or service satisfies customer requirements and expectations.

Value: A customer's ascribed importance of a product or service for satisfying its requirements.

Value stream: The operations and activities from the beginning of a process, such as placing an order, to its completion, such as delivery to the customer.

Value stream map: A graphical display of the routing of materials, information, and other resources through the operations and activities of a process until a customer receives a product or service.

Value stream mapping: Actions taken to build a value stream map.

Value-added: The operations and activities within a value stream that a customer is willing to pay for, such as during design and delivery of a product or service.

Variance: The difference between planned and actual performance.

Verification: Testing a component, product, or service to determine whether it meets certain standards.

Visual control: Indicators, visible to stakeholders in the value stream, displaying the performance status of a system, operation, or product.

Voice of the customer: (1) Collecting the explicit and implicit needs, wants, desires, and expectations of the customer; (2) the results are then translated into requirements and specifications.

Wants: Nice to have requirements that are not necessary to achieve the vision of the project but would please a customer.

Waste: (1) Operations or activities generating output that provides no value to the customer; (2) refer to non-value-added.

Work breakdown structure (WBS): A hierarchical decomposition of a deliverable or deliverables and activities performed on a project.

Work cell: A multidisciplinary, cross-functional arrangement of people, machines, and other resources to produce a product or service.

Workout session: A meeting held on a specific topic to develop solutions to a specific problem or problems affecting a process.

Zero setup: An instantaneous changeover that does not interrupt the flow of a process.

Index

Printed in the United States
by Baker & Taylor Publisher Services